THE BO   .
THE LANDS WE SHARE

THE BORDERS:
THE LANDS WE SHARE

Landscape and life in Scottish and English border country

Andrew Bibby

GRITSTONE
PUBLISHING

For Anoushka and Isaac

Published in 2025 by

Gritstone Publishing Co-operative Ltd.,
Birchcliffe Centre, Hebden Bridge HX7 8DG.

www.gritstonecoop.co.uk

© Andrew Bibby 2025

The author can be contacted via his website www.andrewbibby.com

All photographs © Andrew Bibby, except Hexham Abbey © Jane Scullion

ISBN 978-1-913625-13-9

CONTENTS

CHAPTER I

EDINBURGH CASTLE

Making a start

Walks have to start somewhere. My walk began at Edinburgh Castle.

I mingled with the hordes of visitors by the ticket barrier at the top of the Royal Mile but didn't go inside the castle. I had a hefty pack on my back and there was no obvious place I could see to store it. Anyway I wasn't feeling particularly touristy. I had many miles ahead of me and I wanted to be on my way. So I took a souvenir selfie on my mobile phone with the castle as backdrop and left it at that.

The plan I'd made was to walk south, down through the Scottish border lands. The route was going to take me cross-country, passing on the way through the historic burghs of Peebles, Selkirk, Melrose and Jedburgh, until eventually I reached the Cheviots and found the border into England. It would, according to one of the route-plotting websites I looked at online, work out at around a hundred miles of walking. I had put aside six and a bit days to get there.

And then, after that, I would carry on. The idea I suppose was based on some sort of sense of symmetry: a hundred miles in Scotland and then a similar distance making my way slowly southwards through the English countryside. A chance to see the landscapes on both sides of the border line.

So: thirteen days' backpacking with a little one-person tent and with a total distance of a couple of hundred miles or so to cover (it ended up slightly more). My itinerary said that for some of those days I would necessarily be tackling at least twenty miles of walking. A few days would also see a fair amount of up and down (the Pentland Hills, the Cheviots, the North Pennines). But as this was to be a journey to be enjoyed I also had some shorter days' walking scheduled in: an afternoon off now and again for sightseeing or just relaxing seemed like a good plan.

Walking has its own rhythm, and it's a slow rhythm. Walking allows you the time you need, it allows you to absorb what you see. The rest of the world may be charging about frantically around you but after a day or two of steady walking life settles down to a simpler, quieter pace.

I walked alone. Nothing very terrible happened. I may have got lost once or twice, but only very slightly. The tent didn't collapse. My walking shoes were comfortable. The weather was kind. (In fact, the weather was worryingly good: we're warned to expect more extreme weather and I had chosen a fortnight which turned out to be very hot indeed, with an almost complete absence of rain.)

So, you may be thinking, not much of a story here. No big adventures.

But that's not really what I'm offering. To get to know a landscape is best done on foot, and my intention in tackling this walk was exactly that – to try to understand better how and why the Scottish and English borderlands look the way they do.

'Landscape' has been defined as the result of the interaction of humans with the underlying land forms. Humans have been changing our landscapes all the time that we have been here on earth, in our efforts to survive, find food and prosper. Today's landscapes are not the same as those in times past, and the way we shape the lands will undoubtedly change again in the future. They are moulded by us to meet our current needs and to reflect our current concerns.

In 2006 Britain signed up to something called the European Landscape Convention, an initiative not of the European Union but of the much larger Council of Europe. It was a commitment by our government (and by the other 39 states that also signed up) to look after our landscapes, on the basis that they are important to us – on the basis, in fact, that they form a part of the identity that we draw on as individual human beings and as societies. To quote from the Council of Europe, "the Convention is based on the assumption that landscape is a key element of individual and social well-being everywhere, an essential component of human beings' surroundings and an important part of their quality of life".

What this is saying is that landscape doesn't mean a pretty view – or maybe it can, but it means rather a lot more than that. Understanding the landscape involves, I'd suggest, looking at how we use the land economically, how we arrange the ownership of the land, how we travel about the land, how we interact with nature, how and why we decide to make changes to the land, and – of course – how we use the land for recreation and to bring us pleasure.

My intention in this book is to try to tackle issues like these. This has meant that my thirteen days out on the moors and meadows of the borderlands were only the first part of what I've needed to do. After my walk was over, when I'd safely got home, had done all the washing and had tidied away the tent ready for another day, I started a second, longer, journey of discovery, one that involved being indoors much more than outside. It meant time spent with books and reports and documents, with visits to libraries and with trawls of websites. It meant interviews with a wide variety of people who I felt had insights to offer me (and who all, very kindly, agreed to help me). It was only after this second journey of mine was over that I felt I had something to share, a book which I hope begins to provide a way to read the landscapes of this particular part of our island.

I have chosen for part of the title of the book *The Lands We Share*, but the question has to be asked: in what sense are lands that lie on both sides of a border line 'shared'? My walk took me through two political jurisdictions – indeed, this made my work rather more challenging than it might have been, because I needed to get to grips with two different legislative systems, two different political cultures and to an extent two different ways that local communities are trying to actively intervene to work for change. So my title isn't a rejection of the obvious border division. Don't think that this is an attempt to assert some sort of post-colonial English hegemony over lands that have long been Scotland's.

No, the sharing I have in mind is of a different kind. Certainly I felt I was sharing the land while I was walking through it with those for whom it plays a significant role in their lives – those who live and work here, for example. I had the privilege to explore landscapes that others perhaps more legitimately can claim to know and enjoy.

I was also sharing the lands I walked through with other life – with all the mammals and birds and insects and plants which have their habitats here. I probably should have been more observant of them than I was. Much of the nature that was there I think I took too much for granted – as we often do.

However there is perhaps another sense I had in mind when choosing my title. I don't think it's possible to write a book about landscape today without also being aware of the potentially existential challenges that face humanity at the moment, challenges which do not respect human-made boundaries or divisions. We have a shared climate crisis to contend with. As I discovered, global warming is already having direct consequences in the way that aspects of the border land are currently being shaped. And we face a second potential catastrophe too, that of biodiversity loss. These are issues which we have to tackle together. Shared work.

I'd chosen Edinburgh, and more precisely Edinburgh Castle, to start my walk. I needed to choose my destination, somewhere that was a hundred miles or so south of the border. I got down to the planning and the route took shape: I would cross Northumberland and County Durham and get to Yorkshire before ending my walk. More precisely, I would end my walk on a river bridge. Rivers were going to be important landmarks on my walk and I would be meeting and crossing in turn the Tweed, Yarrow, Teviot, Tyne, Wear, and the Tees. My final river would be the Swale, I decided. I would end my walk on an historic bridge over the Swale: Catterick Bridge, on the old Great North Road.

Maybe I had another reason for choosing to walk from Edinburgh to Catterick. Call it a whim. It relates to a very old poem from this island of ours which is called *Y Gododdin* and which dates back to that period in our history that we often dismiss too readily as the 'Dark Ages'. Somehow I feel that it's altogether too complicated to try to explain all this now, before you've read more than a handful of pages, so the details can come later. I'll save my explanation until my journey is well under way – let's say, until I'm getting close to the Scottish and English border.

But first I have to start walking. I turn my back on Edinburgh Castle and leave the visitors behind. I turn south off the Royal Mile. I pass the imposing National Museum of Scotland. I make my way down across The Meadows. I pass the Royal Observatory.

I'm heading out, towards the edge of the city and into open country.

CHAPTER 2

PENTLAND HILLS

The right to wander

The first full day's walking.

I had camped overnight at Edinburgh's main city campsite near the ring road and was looking forward to getting properly out into the hills. I got the tent folded and into my backpack and started out early, at a time when only dog-walkers were abroad. My route for the day ahead was already carefully planned: I was making a bee-line for the Pentland Hills.

The Pentland Hills may be said to lie at the very gates of the City of Edinburgh. Or so reads part of the first sentence of a very early guidebook for walkers, one which first came out in 1885 with the determined aim of persuading Edinburgh citizens to get out and explore the beautiful countryside on their doorstep. Its author was Walter Smith and his guidebook, small enough to be slipped into the pocket of your hiking jacket, offered a selection of walking routes criss-crossing the range of the Pentlands. "There is no city in Europe that possesses in greater degree than Edinburgh so ready privileges of delightful rural recreation such as this," Smith wrote, perhaps a little provocatively. And yet, he went on, "how comparatively few of even the most active of the sons and daughters of our ancient town have penetrated to their sweet pastoral glens, or crossed their uplying moors and heard the curlew's cry across the heather!"

Smith's book came complete with advice on exactly which rural railway branch line to take out of Edinburgh and which station or halt to alight at, how to make your way into the hillsides to find the best views back over the city and the Forth, and how to ensure you found the finest swards of "delicious turf bejewelled with dainty daisies". In the years after 1885 the guidebook went into numerous reprints and re-editions and more than thirty years later it could still be bought by would-be walkers from its Edinburgh publishers' bookshop in Princes Street.

Walter Smith had an ulterior motive, however, in bringing out his guidebook. At the time of its first publication he was the Acting Secretary of an organisation called the Scottish Rights of Way and Recreation Society, set up to defend the right to walk historic footpaths through the Scottish countryside. The Society under a previous name had had an early success as far back as the 1840s in a tussle over access between the Duke of Atholl and a group of student naturalists led by their Botany Professor from Edinburgh University in the mountain country bordering the Cairngorms. The so-called Battle of Glen Tilt (Glen Tilt is to the north of Blair Atholl) ended in lengthy legal proceedings and has since been seen as a landmark episode in the history of access in Scotland.

By 1885 the Scottish Rights of Way and Recreation Society had decided that walkers needed more help and encouragement to walk in potentially contested areas of countryside. In May that year its committee agreed to spend funds on cast-iron footpath signs to mark footpath routes and some thirty of these new signs were earmarked for paths across the Pentland Hills. There seems to have been an element of direct action involved, as it would appear that landowner consent was not always sought before the signs were erected. It would also seem that not every landowner welcomed the initiative: the Society's minutes for December 1885 reported that two of the cast-iron signs had already been destroyed.

Smith himself implies that there was resistance to the presence of walkers from some landowners at this time. Giving directions for a walk on the western flank of the Pentland Hills near East Cairn Hill, he praises one property-owner for their enlightened attitude but then adds in brackets: *Would that all lairds were as considerate as he!* A short time later in fact Smith was to find himself at the centre of a major dispute over access rights when he led an expedition to signpost rights of way between Braemar and Glen Doll in The Mounth area of the Grampians and was confronted by the keepers of the landowner, Duncan Macpherson. Once again the issue of access was subject to lengthy court proceedings and was only ultimately resolved by the-then highest court in the land, the House of Lords. The Lords found in favour of the Society and the route (named Jock's Road after a local shepherd Jock Winter who had been supporting the Society) is now a popular high-level route for hillwalkers. Nevertheless the court case left the Society (and reportedly the landowner too) virtually bankrupt. It is perhaps not surprising that Smith ended his guidebook with a forthright plug for the Society and its work: "it is hoped all readers of these pages will become Members," he wrote. Membership was £1, but you could pay in instalments.

One of Smith's active colleagues in the Scottish Rights of Way and Recreation Society was a man called James Bryce who from his position as an MP in Parliament was to lead a long campaign for access rights to Scottish mountains and moorlands. Bryce first presented his Access to Mountains (Scotland) Bill in 1884, at a time when he was MP for the perhaps unlikely constituency of Tower Hamlets in east London. His Bill was considerably broader than the aim simply of defending traditional rights of way: he wanted what we would now call the right to roam freely over Scotland's mountains and moorlands.

His 1884 Bill got nowhere at Westminster so Bryce tried again in 1888 (by which time he had moved to be the MP for the rather more appropriate seat of South Aberdeen). This Bill did get a Second Reading, it would appear more by luck than anything else, but again got no further. So, nothing daunted, Bryce presented almost the same Bill four years later, in 1892.

His argument each time was that his proposed legislation was simply restoring a right which Scottish people had long previously enjoyed. "There is no such thing in the old custom of this country as the right to exclusion for purposes of the mere pleasure of the individual; and there is no ground in law or reason for excluding persons from a mountain," he told his fellow MPs when presenting his 1892 Bill. "Eighty years ago everybody could go freely wherever he desired over the mountains and moors of Scotland."

Bryce was many things during his career: an author, a barrister, a Professor of Civil Law at Oxford, a Cabinet minister under Gladstone and, later, from 1907-1913 the British Ambassador to the United States. But he was also a very keen climber and mountaineer. He was part of that generation of middle-class Alpinists from Britain who made the most of the new travel opportunities to the Alps, and indeed he was President of the Alpine Club from 1899 to 1901. Bryce's climbing also took him much further afield: to Iceland in 1872, Mount Ararat in 1879,

Hawaii and the Rockies a little later, and even later in life to Japan. Mount Bryce in British Columbia is named after him.

Scottish access law at the time when Bryce was presenting his Bills was certainly somewhat ambiguous and the law of trespass in Scotland was subtly less hostile to walkers than the position south of the Border. By tradition landowners tended to allow what one Scottish law academic has recently described as "a precarious freedom of access" to hills and mountains. However Bryce was right that the nineteenth century had seen a much more hard-line approach being taken by many Scottish landowners, the result of the development of deer-stalking as a significant sporting industry during this time. What was happening at the time when Bryce was presenting his access Bills in Westminster was something of a clash between two different visions of the way that the Scottish highland landscapes could be enjoyed for middle-class and upper-class recreation, with those wanting to pop away at stags and hinds being challenged by those who were climbers, hillwalkers and naturalists.

However Bryce's Bills faced opposition in Westminster not only from landowners and their representatives but also perhaps more surprisingly from some in the Scottish mountaineering fraternity, particularly from some members of the Edinburgh-based (and respectable) Scottish Mountaineering Club. One SMC member, J. Parker Smith, was an MP for a Glasgow constituency at the time and he criticised Bryce in 1891 for making "an attack upon one class of her Majesty's subjects who use the mountains of Scotland for the recreation of sport, on behalf of another class of her Majesty's subjects who would use the same mountains for the recreation of climbing". The SMC approach seems to have been to have a quiet gentlemanly word beforehand with landowners when planning an excursion. It worked for them, so why was Bryce trying to stir things up?

As in 1884 and 1888, Bryce's 1892 Bill duly failed to reach the statute book. So did his next attempt in 1898. Thereafter, in 1900, a very similar Bill was introduced by his younger brother Annan who was also an MP... and it failed. Annan Bryce tried again with Bills in 1905, 1908 and 1909. They all failed as well.

Indeed, as committed walkers and ramblers know all too well, the issue of access to open countryside, in England and Wales as well as in Scotland, remained unfinished business throughout the whole of the twentieth century. There were regular rallies, there were protests, there was deliberate trespass, there was political lobbying, but England and Wales had to wait until the Countryside and Rights of Way Act of 2000 made it on to the statute book for anything like a 'right to roam'. The CRoW Act, steered through Parliament by the then Labour Environment Minister Michael Meacher, meant that the 'Private' signs which had previously been a feature of much upland moorland had to come down. However the CRoW Act also involved expensive (and controversial) mapping of access land and it remains for many walkers unfinished business: there is no automatic legal right south of the Border to enjoy woodland, lowland countryside or inland waterways, for example.

Scotland had to wait three years after CRoW for the Scottish Parliament to pass its 2003 Land Reform Act but when it came it finally put on a legal basis that traditional de facto right of access that James Bryce had tried to lay claim to. A landmark piece of legislation from the newly (re)established Scottish Parliament which was perhaps enjoying flexing its muscles (and looking for inspiration across the North Sea to the very enlightened land access rights in Scandinavian countries), the 2003 Act offers the legal right to enjoy all of Scotland's land, lowland countryside as well as Highland mountain and moor.

So what were my rights as I walked from Edinburgh south to the Cheviots? Under the 2003 Act I could roam as I chose at will, albeit with sensible exceptions for areas such as private gardens, sports fields, cultivated farmland, airfields, military bases and the like. I had the right to wild camp. I could have brought a bike and cycled or come on a horse and ridden. I could have brought a hang-glider or even carried a kayak and paddled my way down the Borders rivers (not enough room for it in the rucksack, though).

My rights under the Act came with certain responsibilities. Fair enough: I had a duty to care for the environment, to take responsibility for my own actions and to respect the interests of other people using the land. But the owners of the land I crossed had responsibilities too, including the duty to respect my right to walk their land and to have a safe and enjoyable visit.

Backing up the powers of the Act is the comprehensive Scottish Outdoor Access Code, a model of good sense which was brought out in 2005 under the auspices of Scottish Natural Heritage (or NatureScot, as it prefers to be called now). It has taken time, a very long time, since a Times editorial in March 1884 argued that "surely the lords of the soil cannot claim so absolute a monopoly of earth's surface and of the most beautiful parts of it, as wholly to shut out the poor holiday folk, the artist, the naturalist... Surely the many have rights as well as the few." In the end, though, Scotland has got there.

However in just one respect walkers are disadvantaged in Scotland compared with the situation further south. For over fifty years Ordnance Survey has shown on its 1:25,000 and 1:50,000 maps the footpaths, bridleways and byways in England and Wales that are rights of way under the post-War National Parks and Access to the Countryside Act. But this part of the Act doesn't apply north of the Border. Long-distance and certain other popular walking trails in Scotland are shown by OS, but by no means all waymarked routes and paths are marked. As for more local footpaths, these may or may not show up. The Ramblers Scotland charity have tried their best to make up for this deficiency with a very comprehensive Scottish Paths Map which can be consulted online but I'm not sure that's adequate compensation for those of us brought up on traditional map-reading with paper maps in our pockets. If I were Ramblers Scotland I'd be doing some serious lobbying of OS to remedy the situation.

Still, there's not a problem when it comes to the Pentland Hills. After crossing the Edinburgh by-pass I turned off the main road into Hillend Country Park and skirted my way south, through the attractive Erraid Wood and then past the Iron Age hill fort of Castlelaw. At the Flotterstone visitor centre I stopped for a welcome cup of coffee and a fried egg sandwich, and from then on the hills really began.

Walter Smith's cast-iron signs have long gone but you barely need a waymark these days to point you along the footpath that heads up from Flotterstone along the southern range of hills in the Pentlands. A steady stream of people were with me as I made my way up a thousand feet or so of climb to the first of the summits, Turnhouse Hill. After that there was a rapid descent before another climb to the second of the two hills, Carnethy Hill. Walter Scott praised this stretch of hillside in his Journal in November 1827: "I think I never saw anything more beautiful than the ridge of Cairnethy (sic) against a clear, frosty sky... The hills glowed like purple amethysts," he wrote.

Scott's use of the older spelling of Carnethy Hill, incidentally, is one that Walter Smith also copied. It's a reminder that the people who lived in these lands before they were speaking Scots or English spoke an early version of Welsh. Until Edinburgh and the Lothian lands were taken over by Germanic-speaking Angles from Bernicia in the early seventh century the local kingdom was a Celtic one. Their linguistic heritage remains in many place names in the Borders: Carnethy is usually taken as coming from the Welsh for cairns *carneddau* (although the 'car' prefix is also suggestive of *caer*, a castle or fort). Later my walk would take me to another reminder of those speakers of Welsh: Peebles' name comes from *pebyll*, still the modern Welsh word for tents.

Carnethy Hill has given its name to one of Scotland's premier hill-running clubs, the Pentland Hills being the local playground for the club's runners. It somehow *feels* like this hill should be the highest summit of the range. But no, that honour belongs to the next summit on the ridge, Scald Law, which at 579m is just a few metres higher than Carnethy. Once again it's a matter of following the footpath downhill, losing much of the height painfully gained, before starting another brisk climb. By this stage the crowds of fellow-walkers who had accompanied me from Flotterstone were definitely thinning out.

After Scald Law I carried on to two further summits, East Kip and West Kip, before beginning the final slow descent off the hills towards the small settlement of Nine Mile Burn. Walter Smith came this way too: "We pause and admire the pretty view to the south across the valley of the Esk," he told his readers. As he pointed out, this route off the hills is an ancient route known as the Monk's Road with a "curiously hollowed stone called the Font Stone" to be found about half way down. More than a century on from when Smith was writing his guidebook this stone (usually now given its Scots' name of Font Stane) remains in its place among the cropped grass, looking indeed very like a font in a church. In fact it is probably the base of what was once an ancient cross.

Smith was able to invite his readers to stop in Nine Mile Burn for a pint of beer in the "quaint old hostelry" to be found there. No such luck for me – the pub has long gone. No chance either of a drink at the next pub Smith recommends, in the nearby village of Carlops, for this has gone too (although much more recently). So it was on instead to the "pleasant little inn at the north end of West Linton". I'm pleased to say that the Gordon Arms was open, and welcoming.

Walter Smith, an actuary by profession, was to remain actively involved in the outdoor movement. He became in due course the Chairman of the Scottish Rights of Way Society (which remains active today using the shortened name of ScotWays) and went into print again in the 1920s with his book *Hill Paths, Drove Roads and 'Cross Country' Routes in Scotland*. He would, I feel, have been pleased at his legacy.

He would, for example, surely feel that the Pentland Hills today are properly appreciated by very many people from Edinburgh and beyond. The area is officially designated as a Regional Park, a step or two down perhaps from a proper National Park but still requiring its own detailed management plan to ensure that visitor, conservation and landowner interests can be adequately addressed. The formal responsibility for looking after the Regional Park rests with staff of Edinburgh City Council but, as in Walter Smith's day, there is plenty of opportunity for voluntary endeavour to make a difference. The Friends of the Pentlands are a local environmental charity that among other things run work parties several times a month, undertaking tasks such as checking on waymarking posts and repairing stiles and gates. (The Friends have also been responsible for designating a twenty-mile route the length of the hills as the Pentland Way.) Another group has taken on responsibility for making life easier for walkers in the countryside just beyond the Pentlands, including the land around Carlops and West Linton. North Tweeddale Paths was set up in 2001 to be in their own words "the caretaker of paths and rights of way in our area" and they too have a hands-on approach to their work: "if you see any waymarkers guiding you on your way, any drainage dug, trees, bushes or nettles cut back to unblock paths, chances are that NTP members will have done it," they say. Well done to all.

CHAPTER 3

NETHER STEWARTON

Drovers

In the absence of a nearby campsite I'd decided to treat myself to an overnight stay in the Gordon Arms. Once again I was up early. After all the up and down of the Pentlands the day before I was hoping for something a little gentler. My goal that evening was the valley of the Tweed near Peebles.

Not long into my walk, somewhere south-west of West Linton a few miles beyond Romannobridge and near a farm called Nether Stewarton, I came across an almost indecipherable information board positioned at the side of a lane. This 'interpretation board', to give it the name by which it would be known in official parlance, had certainly copped some weather. Year after year it had clearly had to face all the rain, wind and snow sweeping across from the nearby Cloich Hills. It hadn't coped with its fate particularly well.

A few years back, one day when I was feeling mischievous, I wrote a blog for an outdoors website musing on whether the time had come to do away with the whole interpretation board phenomenon. There they all are, I said, dotted up and down the countryside, eager to inform us about exactly what we need to know before we can properly enjoy the countryside for ourselves. Isn't there something just a little patronising about the whole idea of interpreting the landscape for us in this way?

Perhaps it was time to get rid of the whole bloody lot of them. Or maybe, I compromised, at least to impose a moratorium on plans for any new boards.

Don't necessarily hold me to what I was arguing back then. Nevertheless there is certainly a problem with interpretation boards as they grow elderly. By and large there isn't any agency or individual charged with the responsibility to look after them as the years go by, when as at Nether Stewarton the elements begin to take their toll. Fading, peeling, hard to read interpretation boards speak to me of long-forgotten funding applications where the boards were produced in the first place because grant-funders rather liked the sound of them, but where the grants have been long spent and the organisations behind them have moved on.

In one sense, though, the state of the board at Nether Stewarton was appropriate to its subject matter. It was recounting the story of droving, an occupation which was once a very significant part of Scotland's economy but which has now almost completely disappeared from popular memory. Droving, what's that? A typo perhaps for driving?

Certainly the words droving and drovers (those who did the droving) have disappeared from everyday speech although of course we do still talk about things arriving in droves. Almost certainly when we do we have little idea of what the word originally referred to.

The droves were the long lines of cattle, usually many hundreds strong and sometimes comprising more than a thousand beasts, which made their way south, plodding down through the Borders and then through the North of England and the Midlands until they finally reached their journey's end, typically at Smithfield market in London, ready to be turned into fresh meat. There were droving routes too for cattle coming from Wales into England. As Adam Smith put it in his *Wealth of Nations*, the thing about cattle is that almost uniquely they could "carry themselves to market".

The cattle had an exceptionally long journey to make. Those which came south on the drove roads through the Scottish Borders may have originally come from Caithness or Sutherland, from Ross-shire or Inverness-shire, or from the pasturelands of Aberdeenshire and Scotland's North-East. They may have come from the islands of the Hebrides by boat to the mainland, or they may perhaps have lived the early years of their life on Skye and been made to make the hazardous start to their journey by swimming across the narrow strait of Kyle Rhea to reach the mainland. By the time these streams of cattle had reached the Borders they would have been joined by cattle from other parts of Scotland, including the Argyle peninsula and from Galloway. Slowly but steadily they would at this stage by heading south to cross the Border either into Northumberland or Cumberland.

Shortly after I had come down from the Pentland Hills, just before

I reached my overnight stop at West Linton, I had met up with the long-distance path now given the name of the Cross Borders Drove Road. The path (promoted as one of 'Scotland's Great Trails') starts south of Livingston, goes through Peebles and Yarrowford and ends its journey at Hawick. It was going in the direction I wanted to go and as I would choose to stay on it for much of the next two days I clearly needed to find out more about the story behind its name.

We know what we know about droving in Scotland primarily thanks to one man, the lawyer and landowner A.R.B. Haldane, whose 1952 book *The Drove Roads of Scotland* is now rightly regarded as one of the great classics of Scottish history. Haldane himself begins his book by explaining how he first became interested in his subject: "During the autumn of 1942 I had occasion, in the course of certain work on which I was then engaged, to call to mind an old road which crosses the Ochils immediately behind my home near Auchterarder in Perthshire," he wrote. "Little used as it now is, the grassy road retains the clear marks of extensive use by the traffic of former days, and it occurred to me that it would be of interest to try to trace something of its history."

Haldane's first enquiries identified his track as one which had been particularly used by drovers, and so, as he put it, he "determined, as opportunity offered, to get to know more of this droving traffic". From his initial curiosity in one short stretch of trackway emerged an extremely scholarly and comprehensive historical account of the Scottish droving trade and its effect on the landscape.

Although the practice of droving cattle to markets has a long history, the most important period in Scotland was the century and a half between the union of the English and Scottish parliaments in 1707 (after which cross-border trade became rather more straightforward and somewhat safer) and the middle of the nineteenth century. As Haldane puts it, "Were the progress of the Scots droving trade after the Union of 1707 to be illustrated by means of a graph, it would be seen that the index line, after a relatively slow ascent in the first half of the eighteenth century, rose from the middle of the century with increasing steepness to reach its peak about 1835, and that its descent was short, sudden and complete". Long-distance droving did in fact continue into the very start of the twentieth century but by this stage it was very much a dying way of life. Effectively droving disappeared early in Queen Victoria's reign.

One of the achievements of Haldane's painstaking research was his map of Scotland showing in detail the routes taken by the drovers to bring their cattle south through the mountain passes to the Scottish lowlands. Originally the routes converged on the Perthshire market town of Crieff, which was the venue for a major cattle fair (the 'Crieff Tryst') where the cattle would be bought and sold and prepared for the long haul down into England. From about the 1770s, however, the location for the fair moved south to Falkirk, and from then on the Falkirk Tryst was without doubt the place where you had to be if your business was droving or cattle-dealing. Vast numbers of cattle were assembled just outside the town. Haldane quotes a 1777 report which claimed that more than 50,000 animals had been brought together there, and by the early nineteenth century (by which time three separate Falkirk Trysts were being held, in August, September and October) there were reportedly 20,000-30,000 cattle just for the October gathering alone. Sheep were droved too, and would have been there in large numbers. The trysts became major social occasions with something of a carnival atmosphere but they were also crucial to Scotland's economy. Indeed Haldane claims that Falkirk was one of the most important yearly events in the commercial life of Scotland at this time.

We know that by the early years of the nineteenth century more than 100,000 head of cattle (and perhaps as many sheep as well) left Scotland for England every year and almost all of them would have come down from the Falkirk Tryst through the pass in the Pentland Hills known as the Cauldstane Slap on what is now the Cross Borders Drove Road. A little further south (at Romannobridge in fact) there was a route choice facing drovers, when some of the great stream of cattle would have been taken off south and west towards the Annan valley on their way to Carlisle. Later again, at Peebles and Selkirk, there were other possible route choices which drovers could make, depending on whether they were planning to head towards the west or the east of the Pennines. But for a short distance near the Pentland Hills and West Linton almost all the drove roads came together. You'd have certainly known it hereabouts if a drove was coming your way.

What about the people who had the responsibility of ensuring that the cattle and sheep reached their destination? The drovers' work was anything but straightforward: "To purchase 1,000 cattle from a multitude of individuals and march them, in one or more great battalions, from the extremity of Scotland, into the centre of England, at the expense of only a few shillings on each, is an undertaking that requires genius, exertion and a provision for many contingent circumstances," wrote an author in 1813. It was indeed an undertaking where much could go wrong.

There was the basic requirement to ensure that the livestock stayed together, kept going in the right direction and arrived at their destination not only still alive but sufficiently fit and healthy to make a good price when they eventually came to market. Drovers tended in general, and with good reason, not to push their charges too hard and daily mileage was modest, at perhaps ten to twelve miles. At night-time the animals would be turned loose in 'stances' beside the droveways, a suitable stance being perhaps an enclosed field or perhaps simply an open valley or hillside. Sometimes there might be overnight accommodation for the men in a droving inn but it appears that it was much more common for the drovers to bed down in the open alongside their beasts. This also helped protect against straying animals or would-be thieves. Drovers must have been used to a tough life. Walter Scott in one of his stories commented on the paucity of their diet: "a few handfuls of oatmeal and two or three onions", although he also mentioned that this could be washed down with a little whisky. Maybe there was sometimes a little extra, perhaps some ewe's milk cheese to augment the rations, but nevertheless it was not much to survive on during the long journey south.

Haldane suggests that there would have been one herdsman for each fifty to sixty animals, and he adds, "Besides the actual drivers of the cattle, a drove of 200 to 300 animals might have a 'topsman' whose duty it was to go on ahead, usually on horseback, to arrange for grazing for the night and generally to plan the route". Route choice was a key requirement for drovers. Efforts would be taken to avoid where possible the charges levied on toll roads and toll bridges, and also to keep away from hard surfaces which could cause serious damage to the cattle's hooves. Sometimes road surfaces meant that cows were required to have shoes for their hooves, specially made and fitted by blacksmiths. This was an extra expense for drovers to meet and it was also a potentially hazardous undertaking. Unlike horses who can be persuaded to lift their hooves up when they are being shod cattle had to be thrown on to their backs and held down when the shoes were being applied. Each cow's hoof, being cloven, required two separate shoes.

Livestock was also at risk from infectious diseases, generally collec-tively known at the time as murrain or distemper. During outbreaks of disease large numbers of animals could die on their way to market. Haldane recounts a tragic tale from 1745 of a Scottish drover called Thomas Bell, whose drove of over a thousand cattle was severely affected by disease as he made his way through England, leaving him a thousand pounds in debt and "not a shilling to pay it with". Other drovers similarly affected were running away from their diseased cattle, leaving the beasts to die by themselves in the highways, or so Bell wrote to an associate at the time.

Added to the natural risks were the human dangers, particularly the danger of robbery. For centuries, in the heyday of the reivers, much of the Scottish Borders had been a paradise for cattle thieving, as indeed had Highland areas of Scotland too. Old traditions died hard and drovers must have been keenly aware of areas of the countryside where they could have been at risk. There are written sources from the first half of the eighteenth century which make it clear that protection money was paid on occasions to ensure safe passage.

Theft was an obvious risk too for drovers on their return journey north, particularly if they had to bring with them the full value of the livestock in cash. One poor drover was robbed of the enormous sum of £144 7s in Westmorland in the summer of 1692, according to a local court report unearthed by another historian of droving, K. J. Bonser. But droving was not an activity generally based on the cash economy and as the droving trade developed so did an embryonic banking system using promissory notes and bank notes. Local and regional banks were an important presence at the Falkirk Tryst. Credit, often advanced in enormous sums, lubricated the business. Drovers became used to paying farmers for their cattle primarily in credit notes (which would then in turn circulate as a form of currency), with only a small element of hard cash being involved. This was all very well as long as credit could be repaid and as long as the banks did not collapse, but collapse was what banks in the eighteenth and early nineteenth centuries did all too regularly. So the financial basis of the droving business offered yet another hazard to be overcome.

Given all the difficulties it might seem extraordinary that droving took place, and at such scale, but it did. As Haldane puts it, here was a system of commercial dealing calling for skill, courage and honesty of the highest order; "it is impossible not to recognise the merits and qualities of the men whose work it was," he argues.

Droving developed because of one overarching imperative: the need for the supply of food. London in particular was the market that mattered. Here was a capital city which, in 1700, had a population of 600,000 (a tenth of the English population) and which was expanding extremely fast. By the end of the Napoleonic Wars in 1815, for example, London's population had more than doubled to 1.4m. If hunger was to be avoided – and perhaps the concomitant risk to the state of popular unrest – an adequate supply of fresh meat needed to be provided. This was what kept the droves of cattle continuing to plod their way through much of the length of Scotland and England.

What we are talking about, in other words and using today's terminology, are resilient food supply chains to meet market need. Droving may have gone but the need to ensure that people can find the food they need has not gone away. In fact, our government is all too aware of the crucial importance of the UK food supply chain. These days food has been categorised as one of the thirteen Critical National Infrastructure sectors in the UK, the CNIs being defined as those things "necessary for a country to function and upon which daily life depends". (Other CNIs include such things as energy, water, transport and defence.)

Food security becomes particularly significant when you realise that the United Kingdom today currently imports about 46% of the food we consume. Some of this may be the fruit and veg we have become used to eating out of season (those year-round green beans which are grown in Kenya or the asparagus shoots from Peru we can enjoy in January, for example). Even for mainstream crops which can be grown commercially in Britain, however, only about three-quarters of what we need is home produced.

Walking along the Cross Borders Drove Road trail as I did may seem a long way removed from all this, but in fact today's equivalents of the drovers were not so very far away. The people we rely on to keep the food supply chains resilient these days are the long-distance lorry drivers who as I made my way across the hills were busy taking their vehicles up and down the M74, the A68 and the A1.

In fact the working lives of the men and women who transport our food are perhaps not so very different from the lives as lived by Scottish drovers. Their work self-evidently requires resilience and skill, brings responsibility, and involves being away from home for long periods. As with the drovers, bad weather can bring hazards to confront. Anonymous warehouses where the produce being transported can be loaded and unloaded have taken over the role of the Crieff and Falkirk Trysts and the stances of the drovers are today the lay-bys and service areas where lorries can be parked up overnight. Fundamentally, though, you could argue that the economic driving force behind the long-distance haulage industry is not so far removed from the imperative that drove forward the droving business. (Mind you, I have yet to see an interpretation board explaining to me the way that the long-distance haulage industry works. Maybe it's simply a matter of time.)

We need to complete the story of the drovers properly. A number of things did for their trade in the second half of the nineteenth century. Easier ways of getting cattle to market came along. Steam ships were introduced, transporting the cattle and sheep down the Scottish and English coasts. The rapidly expanding railway network after the 1840s became particularly important.

But there was another more insidious development which attacked the principles on which droving had developed, and that was the growing shift towards a more individualised, privatised attitude to land in the countryside. The enclosure movement, which converted previously communally worked lands into individualised plots, was a phenomenon both in England and Scotland. In England, this process was undertaken through the numerous enclosure Acts which Parliament approved, particularly in the period between the middle of the eighteenth and the middle of the nineteenth centuries. In Scotland, the process was if anything quicker and easier than in England for those promoting the partition of the commons, with the key legislation being the Division of Commonties Act of 1695. By early in the nineteenth century almost all the common land in Scotland had become the private property of nearby (or more distant) landowners.

Enclosure meant that droving as an activity could become, literally, hedged in, the routes available for the drovers to choose being restricted to much narrower tracks between new enclosure boundary hedges or walls. It also meant that land which drovers had previously used as overnight stances was no longer necessarily readily available. Stances had in the early years of droving generally been available without charge (there was a quid pro quo at work here, because land where cattle assembled would be fertilised by their dung). Later, however, there was an increasing tendency for drovers to be required to pay for their use of stances – another expense to be added to all the others.

There was also the development during the nineteenth century of driven shooting of game birds on hill-country estates (that is, the practice of driving birds towards the guns rather than so-called 'walked-up' shooting). The introduction in the 1840s and 1850s of the breech-loading shotgun which enabled sportsmen to kill many more birds more easily reinforced this trend. So began the much more intensive management of moorland areas as shooting estates.

This changing context for droving can be seen as being symbolised by a high-profile legal case in the 1840s, focused on a traditional droving stance south of Rannoch Moor at Inveroran which the landowner Lord Breadalbane wanted to close. The closure affected several long-established droving routes from further north and west, and a group of drovers faced with a serious threat to their trade took the highly significant step of instigating litigation against Breadalbane. Their argument, that their right to the stance came through continued historical unchallenged use, was upheld when the case first came to court. However Lord Breadalbane chose to appeal to the House of Lords and – perhaps not altogether surprisingly – his colleagues in the Lords reversed this judgment and found in his favour. The drovers had no a priori right to what were described as "the profits of the soil", their Lordships resolved.

Of course it is all old history now.

Or just possibly it isn't. As this book was being prepared there was much press interest in the case brought against the Dartmoor National Park Authority by the Dartmoor landowner Alexander Darwall, a hedge fund manager, seeking to outlaw wild camping on his extensive area of moorland. His case was rejected by the Court of Appeal in 2023 but Darwall's lawyers promptly appealed to the highest court in the land (now the UK Supreme Court rather than the Lords) who began considering the case in late 2024. Some arguments over conflicting rights to land usage still echo down today.

CHAPTER 4

ESHIELS WOOD

Community woodlands

The Cross Borders Drove Road dropped me down out of the countryside straight into the north end of the town of Peebles. Once the county town of Peebles-shire, this was the first of the historic Borders burghs to be on my route.

I stopped to pick up supplies for the next day's breakfast at a convenience store in the town, but time was getting on. I had phoned in advance to book my tent in at the popular Glentress walking and mountain biking centre run by Forestry and Land Scotland, but that meant I still had a few more miles to tackle before I could settle in and cook myself my evening meal. Take the old railway path, I'd been told: you can pick it up just beyond the Peebles Hydro.

Once upon a time, as befitting the importance of a Borders burgh, Peebles had three railway lines. You could travel north to Edinburgh up the valley of little Eddleston Water, or you could go west to Biggar following initially the valley of the upper Tweed, or you could go east to Galashiels, this time following the Tweed downstream. But all these lines have gone. The last passenger train rolled out of the town more than half a century ago, the service an early victim of the Beeching-era cuts. Today if you haven't got access to a car you have to pin your faith in the bus.

Disused and derelict railway tracks are one of the aspects of the landscape which we have inherited from the early years of industrialisation. These are the lines which, when they were first opened, would have been greeted with civic pomp and great community celebration. There may have been a few people back then who tut-tutted at the rearrangement of the familiar countryside which railway construction inevitably brought about, but by and large the new lines were seen as a sign of progress and prosperity. It was a good thing to mess around with the landscape to get the railway through. Railways represented a more hopeful future.

It has to be admitted that some of those nineteenth century railway lines were probably always destined to be economic basket-cases, doomed from the start. Their original shareholders should have known better than to have coughed up the investment capital. But on the other hand we now know that some of those railways which at the end of their lives disappeared into history with a whimper were closed unwisely.

We can also regret something else that happened in the great railway closures which climaxed in the 1960s and that was the selling off of the track-beds. Other European countries which also closed their branch lines seem to have handled this differently, leaving the track-beds untouched, presumably on the 'just in case' principle. In our case, all too many former railway lines have had their land (the solum, if you want to be technical) parcelled up and sold off into a patchwork of private ownerships. This means today that potential transport arteries which, even if it weren't to be possible to bring back the railway itself, could at least have been turned into walking and cycle ways have been lost. Recreating them now means re-acquiring the land: almost starting again from scratch.

But the solum of the old North British Railway line between Peebles and Galashiels seems to have managed to escape this fate. And years after the trains had gone the line found itself a new future. In 2009, when money for public investment was rather more available than it has been recently, the Scottish Borders Council and the cycling charity Sustrans put together a proposal to reopen ten kilometres of the track-bed from Peebles as far as Innerleithen as a cycle path. The Tweed Valley Railway Path as it was named opened two years later, in 2011.

At the time the local authority hinted that the ultimate ambition was to extend the path all the way from Peebles through to Galashiels. That has yet to prove possible, although a short additional stretch from Innerleithen to Walkerburn was added in 2019 (and meanwhile another cycle and walking track has recently been created north from Peebles up the Eddleston Water valley).

For me the Railway Path was just what I needed at the end of my day's walking – a pleasant gentle amble offering my first glimpse of the great Borders river, the Tweed, even if at this point it was still quite a young river. And there was another bonus: a mile or two out from Peebles the path led me straight to Eshiels Wood.

Eshiels is a long thin wedge of woodland squeezed in between the old railway route and the Tweed. This little patch of land has been wooded for many years: the first Ordnance Survey map of the area, surveyed in 1856, shows both broadleaf trees and conifers here, and although there has been some felling and replanting in the many years since then the mix of trees remains very similar today. At present about 70% of the woodland is conifer and the remaining 30% is broadleaf. But that's about to change.

It's a wood which in recent years has been well used by local people. Dog walkers come this way and some informal off-road cycle tracks have also developed. There's wildlife here, too, including red squirrels: Eshiels is more or less on the current front line in the battle which red squirrels are waging against their North American cousins the grey squirrels. If you're lucky you may see otters. If you're *very* lucky, you might see a pine marten, a shy mammal which was once widely persecuted but is now making something of a comeback, particularly in woodlands in the Scottish border areas. Visit as the light is fading and there's a chance of spotting another of Britain's mammals, Daubenton's bat. This small creature, sometimes called the water bat, glides low just above the river snatching up insects. (In case you are curious I can advise that the bat carries the name of the eighteenth century French naturalist Louis-Jean-Marie Daubenton.)

So Eshiels Wood is worth exploring. But it's a wood whose future only a relatively short time ago was uncertain. It was run at the time by Forest Enterprise Scotland, what was to become Forestry and Land Scotland, and Eshiels was something of an outlier from the main body of its commercial woodland a short distance away at Glentress, the big forest centre with the campsite I was making for. The agency decided that Eshiels was surplus to requirements and put it on the market.

And so a group of local people sprang into action in an attempt to secure the future of the woodland by taking it into community ownership. Their task was made easier by the fact that the Scottish government has resolved that, in situations like this where public agencies are disposing of property, local communities should have the first opportunity to claim it for themselves. The right to apply for what's known as an asset transfer is enshrined in the Community Empowerment (Scotland) Act of 2015.

But the process of turning Eshiels into a community-controlled woodland was by no means a straightforward undertaking. The legislation doesn't mean that every asset transfer request is automatically granted. First of all, a community group has to demonstrate that it has a strong case. There's an application form of course, with a detailed series of questions for which convincing answers need to be provided: *What evidence has the organisation provided of how it will take into account the different needs of the community, and what contribution will the project make to equalities outcomes? What is the impact of any non-financial benefits, including economic development, regeneration, public health, social wellbeing, environmental wellbeing, inequalities of outcome...? To what extent do the overall vision for the project and the project outcomes contribute to Scotland's National Outcomes?* And so on, over several pages.

For the Eshiels group the application form was just the start. The team of volunteers working on the proposal also had to show that they had undertaken adequate community consultation to demonstrate genuine local support. There was a business plan for the project to submit, a forestry management plan setting out how the woodland would be cared for in community hands, and a habitat report explaining in detail the biodiversity of the land.

So there was a lot of work to undertake before the transfer application was finally submitted in January 2017. But there was also the need to try to find finance for the project, in order to actually buy the woodland. The rights in the Community Empowerment Act don't mean that assets will be transferred free of charge. In the case of Eshiels Wood the price that was agreed was based on the market value of the land but with a discount factored in on conservation grounds because (rather helpfully) a rare moth, the currant shoot-borer, makes the wood its home.

To find the finance an application was made to the Scottish Land Fund. This is the pot of money created to back up the support the Scottish government has been giving since devolution to land reform in Scotland, and in particular to the transfer of land into community custodianship. The Fund's most recent significant grants have been £4.4m given in 2018 to enable the island of Ulva off the coast of Mull to be purchased by a community trust (nearby land on Mull itself was included too) and a grant of £1m in 2022 to the Langholm Initiative, another community venture taking over a large estate of moorland and farmland close to the town of Langholm in Dumfries and Galloway, which I'll mention again a little later. The £1m received by Langholm is now the maximum grant available and some land reformers argue that the Land Fund has become much too small to support significant future community buy-outs of private estates.

Nevertheless what the Land Fund has also been doing has been making more modest grants for smaller-scale community projects: £200,000 to buy two houses in Papa Westray in Orkney for renting out to local families, £150,000 to reopen an empty shop in Gargunnock village in Stirlingshire, £120,000 to buy and restore a pier in Argyll, and so on. And, yes, grants are available for community woodland purchase too.

You will probably have guessed by now that the Eshiels Wood story has a happy ending: the Scottish Land Fund agreed in September 2018 to award a grant to cover both the purchase price and other initial expenses and the asset transfer was approved by Forest Enterprise Scotland. *"Community steps in to save Eshiels woodland"* boasted the headline in one of the local papers shortly afterwards. "The plantation will live on under community ownership", the news story below the headline carried on.

Of course I was unaware of any of this background as I heaved my rucksack past the entrance to the woodland on my way to my campsite that afternoon. But later, when the walk was over and I was safely back home at my desk, I wanted to get the full story. I made contact with the group through their Facebook page and arranged to have a chat with two of their management group members, Alex Wilson and John Woolliams.

We're actually a sub-group of the local community-run development charity Peebles Community Trust, Alex Wilson explained to me. "Peebles is the sort of place where everyone is involved in something, and the advantage of the Trust is that it was already set up and able to back this project," she went on. In fact since the successful take-over of Eshiels Wood the Trust has gone on to tackle other projects, including taking over an empty social club in the town to run as a community centre. Development Trusts like the one in Peebles have become important players in the economic and social regeneration of their communities, in a very people-focused bottom-up sort of way. There are now over three hundred in Scotland.

I pointed out the obvious to Alex and John: acquiring a woodland is, by its very nature, a long-term commitment. Were they convinced that they could ensure it was looked after by the community for very many years to come? Alex told me that, with the Trust as owner, there was now the legal protection in place to ensure this, but she also added that their group has built up a network of active volunteers prepared to come along and get stuck in when work needed doing. "If we need help we just put a call out," she said. And she has also been building up strong links with Peebles' High School and with the local Scouts.

We've got a strong management plan for the wood, John chipped in. The plan in outline is to remove the conifers and to replace them with native broadleaf species. As a start they're doing this little by little, taking down perhaps three or four conifer trees every few months and then passing the wood to a volunteer to store and split ready for selling on locally as firewood. "We've decided that the proceeds from the sale of the firewood will be in aid of the local food bank," John added. It's an indirect way for Eshiels Wood to help those people in Peebles finding themselves in fuel poverty. Longer term, a more extensive felling programme is envisaged.

Once the conifers have all been removed, there will be the opportunity for a big push to involve the community in the necessary new tree planting. And after that the wood should more or less look after itself, John told me. The group's focus will be able to be much more exclusively on recreation and education. Alex is already talking of using QR codes to explain what can be found in the wood, with her sights set on reaching young people via their mobile phones.

Woodlands are important places which we all need to cherish. They are valuable for nature education and conservation. They're good for our physical health and our mental health too. And of course, as we're increasingly realising, we need to ensure that we keep our trees so that they can act as carbon stores, as our planet heats up more and more from global warming. So what is happening in the seven hectares (17 acres)* of Eshiels Wood is an inspiring story.

But it's certainly not unique. Recent years have seen the development of a lively network of community-managed woodlands across Scotland. Nobody has tallied up the full number but around 160 community organisations have chosen to affiliate to the Scottish national body, the

* Hectares or acres? With some uncertainty I have decided to be metric in this book. A hectare is a more logical unit than an acre, being an area which is a hundred metres by a hundred metres. For the equivalent area in acres, multiply hectares by about 2.47.

Community Woodlands Association. The CWA produces publications and offers advice to help new woodland groups get going, and there is also much informal networking and sharing of experiences between the different groups.

The community woodlands movement traces its roots back to a first venture at Wooplaw in the Scottish Borders a few miles north of Galashiels and Tweedbank and therefore only a relatively short distance from Eshiels. It was here in 1987 that a local wood sculptor and furniture maker called Tim Stead raised funds towards what has now become the locally based charity Wooplaw Community Woodlands. The organisation is run entirely by volunteers, who manage the wood for the benefit of locals and visitors. They have established footpaths (including an extensive network of paths suitable for all abilities), built a thatched roundhouse and also created spaces for picnics and barbeques. They want the woodland used for as many events as possible, they say, and they encourage other groups to use it for arts events or for running woodland skills sessions.

Wooplaw's pioneering venture helped bring about the creation of the Community Woodlands Association. Andy Rockall, the CWA's current Director, told me that the majority of CWA member organisations rely just on volunteer effort. But each venture is different, he said. Some groups manage only very small patches of woodland, even as small as the size of a football field, while others – particularly the high-profile community buy-outs of large estates in the Highlands and Islands – may own thousands of hectares of land, although not all of it will necessarily be woodland. There are other differences: about half of the CWA members have ownership of their woodlands but the other half manage the woods under an agreement with the ultimate landowner. "But they're all trying to deliver benefits for their own community, even if the benefits may vary," Andy told me.

I asked him what is the spur that first gets a new community woodland project off the group and he replied that reasons can vary massively. It could be, as in the case of Eshiels, that an existing woodland is on the market and local people want to protect it. Sometimes it may be a desire to prevent land from being developed for housing. Sometimes the main driver can be biodiversity and conservation concerns. One CWA member, Andy told me, is primarily holding a woodland in order to help people with additional support needs get out into the countryside.

But of course, as he went on to point out, the journey that a new group has to take from the early vision to the established reality of community ownership can be a lengthy one. "It's a long journey from being, say, a dog walker wanting to protect a bit of local woodland to actually forming a committee, doing the paperwork, dealing with the legislation, choosing your structure," he said. And it is true that some ventures fall by the wayside. Particularly if the initial push comes in a top-down way, say from a landowner looking to get out of their responsibilities, a community project can feel exploited rather than empowered by the tasks they are expected to take on.

But despite the hard work involved this seems to be a model for woodland landscapes which is making a real difference in many parts of Scotland. Perhaps once upon a time we might have expected local authorities to be the natural agency to look after community landholdings on all our behalf. However the sad decline in funding for local government means that we are increasingly having to do things ourselves.

I left Eshiels Wood behind with some regret. I hadn't seen a pine marten and I certainly hadn't seen the currant shoot-borer moth. But maybe next time.

CHAPTER 5

MINCH MOOR

Commercial forestry

You can't believe everything you read on the Internet. The next morning I set off early, taking the Railway Path onwards to Innerleithen and then following the B-road down to Traquair House. Google told me that the Old Walled Garden café there opened at ten. I was twenty minutes early but decided to wait. I fancied a good strong cup of coffee and maybe something to eat, as a second breakfast to fortify me for the day ahead.

Traquair House is deservedly popular with visitors. Its claim to fame is that it is the oldest inhabited house in Scotland, having been lived in for more than nine hundred years. It has necessarily accumulated over the years its fair share of history. Mary Queen of Scots came visiting in 1566 along with her baby son James, the infant who was to grow up to become James VI (of Scotland) and James I (of England and Wales). Bonnie Prince Charlie probably paid a visit too at the time of the 1745 Jacobite Rebellion. In the years since 1491 there have been 21 Lairds of Traquair, the 21st and latest being a woman, Catherine Maxwell Stuart, who lives in the house with her family today (or at least those bits of the house which she hasn't opened to the public).

The walled garden at Traquair is also worth seeing. I plonked myself and the rucksack down on a garden bench watching the gardener who was hard at work mowing the immaculate lawn, as I waited for ten o'clock to come round.

At about seven minutes past ten I made some enquiries. Oh we open at eleven came the reply, didn't you know? No coffee, no flapjack or rocky road for me this time. I picked up the rucksack and made my way reluctantly down the main drive.

I had briefly left behind the Cross Borders Drove Road route in Peebles but I joined it again in the village of Traquair for the long ascent up on to Minch Moor. At 567 metres the highest point here is only a handful of metres below the height of Scald Law in the Pentland Hills. It felt like a climb. The day was really hot, and I began to ask myself whether I had brought enough water to last out the day.

The track over Minch Moor is famous as an old droving road. Walter Scott wrote a story called *The Two Drovers* in which he has one of his characters a Highlander called Robin Oig trying unsuccessfully to teach his English friend Harry Wakefield the Scots Gaelic for calf. "From Traquair to Murder-cairn, the hill rung with the discordant attempts of the Saxon upon the unmanageable monosyllable," Scott wrote. The story ends tragically (if in a suitably romantic fashion) later on in England with Robin killing his friend Harry as a result of a misunderstanding, pleading guilty to the murder, and accepting his death sentence by hanging. All very Walter Scott. You can read the story for yourself.

I'm not sure where Murder Cairn was to be found on Minch Moor but my guess is that it has long been swallowed up by the commercial forestry which has been planted on the hillsides. The landscape which would have been familiar to Robin Oig and Harry Wakefield, or at least to their non-fictional equivalents who came droving cattle and sheep this way, would have been completely different from the landscape we see today.

The most obvious recent landscape change up on Minch Moor has been the creation of the Elibank and Traquair Forest, which is in the hands of Forestry and Land Scotland and is one of those very extensive stretches of dense commercial forestry made up of non-native conifer species which tend not to be at the top of the list of walkers' favourite walking areas. Blame the First World War, perhaps, and the government's very belated realisation then that the country's timber stocks were almost completely exhausted. After the war in 1919 the government quickly passed the Forestry Act, establishing the Forestry Commission to try to remedy things by buying up agricultural land and planting forests. Farmland at the time was cheap and the Forestry Commission, a government department, rapidly became one of the largest landowners in the country. The state remains a major owner of our commercial forests, public pressure having successfully defeated attempts to privatise the Commission in both 1993 and 2010.

As you might expect, Scotland has proportionately more of Britain's forests as a percentage of overall land cover. Currently about 18.5% of Scotland is forested compared with 13% in Britain as a whole.

But go back far enough and the Scottish landscape was quite unrecognisable from what we can see today. The last Ice Age left Britain only about 10,000-11,000 years ago, a blink of an eye in terms of geological time. Woodland gradually began to spread across the Scottish landmass following the retreat of the glaciers and ice sheets and by around 3000 BCE, five thousand years ago, woods are thought to have covered as much as 60% of the land. Down in the south of Scotland oak was probably the primary species while Scots pines would have been the dominant tree on poorer soils and in the central Highlands. There's nothing 'natural' therefore about Scotland's bare mountain and moorland landscapes which pull the tourists to the Scottish Highlands.

After that the woodland cover gradually diminished. Humans got to work cutting down trees to create fields for crops and for grazing, and then started taking timber in a much more organised way. Wood was needed. Ships needed oak, for example. Country houses were constructed with timber frames. Charcoal was required as a fuel. Wood was a commodity with all sorts of uses.

In more recent times the woods have suffered from overgrazing by sheep, from destruction caused by excessive numbers of deer, and from the demand for grouse moors. By the time that the Forestry Commission was being created in 1919, the percentage of Scotland which was covered by woodland was down to a meagre 4%.

However the Border landscapes today are the result of another dramatic change, once again caused by human agency. This was the devastating period of Land Clearances which took place in the Borders counties at the behest of landowners in the eighteenth and early nineteenth centuries when smaller farmers and labourers lost their homes and livelihoods in order to make way for large-scale sheep farming.

The shocking story of the Highland Clearances has entered deep into Scottish consciousness. By contrast the Clearances in the Borders are much less well known. The historian Tom Devine, whose 2018 book *The Scottish Clearances: A History of the Dispossessed* has rapidly gained the status of a classic, devotes a hundred pages of his book to this earlier history. "Contrary to popular belief, the removal and abandonment of traditional rural communities in eighteenth-century

Scotland did not start in the Highlands," he writes. He talks of a "seemingly inexorable white tide" of sheep which led to the uprooting of many peasant communities in the Borders. It was, he maintains, "a scale of dispossession in the early-eighteenth-century eastern Borders which evokes comparison with the more familiar Highland experience of later decades".

So there is a reason why today a walker will find themselves making their way along the footpaths and tracks through a Borders countryside which, outside the burghs, is almost empty. Tom Devine says that the process of removing the smaller farms and cottages from the land was virtually complete by the time of the Battle of Waterloo in 1815. The landowners may have been stubbornly conservative when it came to politics but in terms of maximising the economic benefits of their land they were revolutionaries, Devine suggests.

And now the Borders landscapes have changed again, with the commercial forestry plantations and (particularly in the west, in Dumfries and Galloway) the arrival of massive wind farms. Commercial forestry is important economically to Scotland. A 2015 report for the Scottish government calculated that the industry was responsible for providing around 20,000 jobs, with a further 6,000 or so created by the exploitation of the forests for tourism and recreation purposes. All told, forestry added not far short of a billion pounds to the Scottish economy.

There are, of course, criticisms of the way that commercial conifer forestry has covered the hills, particularly when it comes to very densely planted conifers with little or no undergrowth. The predominant conifer that is planted, sometimes described as an 'exotic' variety, is the Sitka spruce which originally comes from North America. The Sitka, it turns out, rather enjoys Britain's maritime climate and reaches maturity in a comparatively short time – between 35 and 50 years. After fifty years you'll end up if things go to plan with about 600 or 700 cubic metres of timber for each hectare of your forest. Typically Sitka plantations will be clear-felled in one go at this point (it's much more straightforward and much cheaper than just felling some of the trees), with the land then left bare for a few years before the cycle begins all over again. Sitka makes up around 60% of conifer plantations in Britain, slightly more in the case of the publicly owned forests.

The Forestry Commission became a little more sensitive in its approach to planting following the wave of complaints in the Sixties and Seventies about the dismal appearance of some of its landholdings.

Legislation in 1985 obliged it to try to take account of conservation issues as well as timber production, and an earlier Act, in 1968, started the move towards recreational use of the forests. Forestry and Land Scotland (which along with the regulatory and funding agency Scottish Forestry has taken over the Forestry Commission's roles following devolution) certainly tries to encourage the public use of both the Glentress and the Elibank and Traquair Forests, and there are among other things some challenging mountain biking trails which can be undertaken if you're so minded. I think it's satisfactory too that, while the plantations on Minch Moor cloak the flanks of the hillside, the highest ground has been left unplanted. After the deep shade of the trees as I walked up from Traquair I emerged eventually into the open. A little of the old Minch Moor remains.

Though public ownership is important more than half of Scotland's (and the UK's) commercial forests are privately owned. It's a business which can prove very attractive if you have the wherewithal. This is "a proven asset class which has delivered compelling real returns" as one asset management company puts it in their introductory guide to the sector. Income from forestry is exempt from income tax and corporation tax, and with the right advice you can arrange for any capital gains tax liabilities to be reduced. Commercial forestry (both the trees and the land underneath) normally also qualifies for full relief from Inheritance Tax (IHT). "Forestry offers considerable investment flexibility... This can be accomplished within an environment which provides 100% IHT relief, allowing for flexibility in financial planning," the guide concluded.

Tempted? After all, commercial forestry as we've seen provides jobs and boosts the economy. It also helps to meet our country's requirement for timber and paper, and as a country we of course need timber and wood products. At present only a very small amount of what we use is home-grown. More than 80% of our wood requirements in Britain has to be imported and the UK indeed is the third largest importer of wood products globally, behind only China and the USA. Maybe we need to do rather better. Maybe we do need more forests.

The Scottish government certainly thinks so. Its current national forestry strategy calls for a considerable increase in forest and woodland cover in Scotland over the next fifty years. As it points out, Scotland's 18.5% cover is extraordinarily low compared with many other European countries: Germany has 33% woodland, Norway 40%, Sweden 69% and

Finland 74%. Even southern European countries do better: Spain has 37% of its land forested, Portugal 36% and Italy 33%. Really, in terms of land usage Scotland, and the UK as a whole, is right at the bottom of the table.

Increasing tree cover is seen by the Scottish government as producing several benefits. The minister for rural affairs in the Scottish government at the time when the forestry strategy was launched said that she wanted forestry in Scotland to play a significant role in the rural economy but also help to meet "our ambitions to make Scotland a low carbon economy and a world leader in dealing with the threat of climate change". It's certainly true that up to now the Scottish government has been making somewhat more enthusiastic noises about confronting global warming than the government in Westminster: while the latter has the target of achieving net zero carbon emissions by 2050 (the agreed international deadline under the Paris Agreement) in Scotland the target date has been brought forward to 2045.

It turns out that there has been an active debate going on within at least some parts of civil society in Scotland about exactly how this move towards greater afforestation should be undertaken. Leading the debate has been an organisation called the Forest Policy Group which for twenty years has been pressing for a broader approach to forestry within Scotland, one which takes account of the need to strengthen rural communities and to take proper account of biodiversity and conservation concerns. *Woodland Nation*, a recent report from the group authored by two of its Board members Anna Lawrence and Willie McGhee, can perhaps be read as a sort of manifesto.

"Woodland Nation is a vision of a Scotland where forests cover more than twice their current extent, much of which is natural woodland," they write, "where the land and the forests are part of our society and economy, supporting prosperous rural communities and the wider economy through fairer ownership and attention to the environmental, economic and social benefits…The reforesting of Scotland must be part of a process that leads to more equitable ownership of land, and fairer distribution of the environmental, economic and social benefits of reforestation."

Any far-thinking development of forestry surely needs to address the twin issues of global warming and biodiversity loss together. Perhaps we can learn from elsewhere: Norway was mentioned to me a number of times as an example of a northern European country more conscious

of the need to manage commercial forestry in a sustainable, environ-
mentally-friendly way.

So, as the authors of *Woodland Nation* put it, "the issue is not whether
trees are good, but what kind of trees, and where; and who experiences
them as benefits or disbenefits". Are new forests going to be for the
benefit of society as a whole or are they simply to be a new income
stream for landowners and the forestry industry?

It is perhaps time to explore the economics behind forestry a little
more. Economics may be a dismal science but in any attempt to really
comprehend why our landscapes look the way they do we have to, I
think, explore the underlying economic base behind the way the land
is used. The first thing to say is that, in all nations and regions of the
UK, there are currently government grants designed to encourage the
planting of new woodlands and forests.

The Scottish government has in recent years been helpful in this
respect. If your application is successful, you will currently be eligible
for an initial planting grant, a contribution towards capital costs such as
fencing and tree protectors and then an annual maintenance payment
for the first five years. The grants are higher if you are planning new
broadleaf woodland so that – depending on where in Scotland you want
to plant your trees – you could find yourself at the moment eligible in
total for over £6,000 funding for each hectare of land. Conifer planting
is less generously funded (conifers are more likely to bring in a greater
commercial return) but even here you could be eligible for £3,000-
£4,000 per hectare. In fact, arguably, the Scottish government's keenness
to see new forests planted is in danger of backfiring: shortly after I had
completed my walk through the Borders the government announced
that pressures on its finances meant that the budget it was providing for
the Forestry Grant Scheme was under pressure, particularly for larger
projects. The government has had to admit that for the time being at
least its annual target for new woodland creation will not be met.

However the grants from the Scottish government (and the grant
schemes run in England, Wales and Northern Ireland as well) are just
the icing on the cake if you are seriously thinking of an afforestation
project. Something else has been happening in recent years, something
which has major implications for the way that our upland landscapes
look now and will look in the years to come. This development is
international in its reach and is bringing in major players in the financial
sector. It is carbon offsetting.

I mentioned earlier the targets which the UK and Scottish governments have set to become net zero. This is a term which is much bandied about but which isn't necessarily always understood. The principle is simple: human activity creates carbon and other greenhouse gases which escape into the atmosphere and demonstrably create climatic warming. But there are various ways that these gases can also be *removed* from the atmosphere. Net zero would mean that we had reached that point where the sum of new emissions entering the atmosphere was exactly balanced by the amount of gases being taken out. At that point (assuming we manage to get there, and assuming we get there globally and not just locally) we should have turned the corner on any further global warming.

Of course, far and away the best way of moving towards net zero is to reduce the emissions we are creating in the first place. Removing greenhouse gases in compensation for on-going new emissions is seen by environmentalists and climate scientists as very much a second best. But on the other hand, up to now, the human race (or perhaps it is our way of running our economic system?) seems to be struggling to achieve meaningful reductions.

So at the moment we perhaps need to look also for effective techniques on the other side of the equation. As is well known, trees are one way that carbon can be removed from the atmosphere and stored or 'sequestrated'. During daylight hours the leaves of trees absorb carbon dioxide from the atmosphere and through the process of photosynthesis store some of this as carbon. About half the total carbon is held by a tree in its trunk, with about 25%-35% in the roots and the rest in the branches and leaves.

The amount of greenhouse gases which trees secrete in this way can be calculated. The usual calculations for sequestration are done in terms of tonnes (t) of carbon dioxide (CO_2), with other greenhouse gases (such as methane) converted into 'carbon equivalent' figures. This is very often written in mathematical form as tCO_2e.

This formula can be extended to read $tCO_2e\ ha^{-1}\ yr^{-1}$, which simply means the tonnes of carbon or equivalent stored per hectare per year. So how much do trees store? It's complicated of course, but not surprisingly it's an area of study which many scientists have been undertaking recently. Indeed if you take a trip to the right woodland you will be able to see curious metal structures ('flux towers') which have been assembled over the canopy of the trees, designed to measure exactly the net CO_2 retained by trees (this is the difference between the carbon dioxide intake during daytimes and the carbon dioxide emitted by trees during darkness). Other ways of measuring carbon sequestration by trees are also being tried out, including a technique known as terrestrial laser scanning.

A mature forest that's been well managed and periodically thinned is likely to have several hundred tonnes of CO_2e stored in its trees per hectare but the exact amount of carbon sequestration depends on the type of trees, the soil, the forest management undertaken and many other factors. The amount is anyway probably irrelevant for our purposes. The key thing is that, because the calculation can be done, the carbon held in trees – or the potential carbon to be held in trees which are planned to be planted – can be monetised and commoditised.

Carbon trading has been in operation since the end of the last century between individual countries so that for example developed countries can buy credits from other countries to count towards their own emission reduction targets. This can be seen as a nifty way to tie the requirement to reduce global warming into the workings of a globalised economy, although it has to be said that local populations in developing countries have frequently been asking what precisely the benefits have been for them. But carbon trading has extended since those early days, and in particular what has developed more recently is the so-called voluntary carbon market. A large company such as, say, a supermarket chain or an airline which wants to demonstrate that it is environmentally concerned can do so by acquiring the right to units of stored carbon to set against its own emissions. It is this market which is creating opportunities for trading carbon stored in new forests.

There are difficulties in the concept of trading carbon: there is the inherent risk of the carbon stored in trees being inaccurately calculated, either inadvertently or through general dodgy practice. It's also a fact that it takes a long time for trees to sequestrate carbon, and lots of people want to be able to trade that future carbon immediately. In fairness it has to be said that the government has taken steps to try to meet both these concerns through the establishment in 2011 of the Woodland Carbon Code. It is the Woodland Carbon Code which offers a standard methodology for working out how much carbon a particular new afforestation project will store. (There are online spreadsheets to help you.) The Code also provides verification mechanisms for ensuring that proposed trees do get planted and do get looked after. There's a national Register of UK Land Carbon projects, with exact details of the location and ownership of each venture. There is, therefore, a relatively robust framework established on which voluntary carbon trading can take place.

Ingeniously, too, the Woodland Carbon Code offers a way round the difficult fact that trees are unfortunately just so s-l-o-w to grow. For newly established forests the Code enables you to trade something known as Pending Issuance Units (PIUs), or effectively carbon I-O-Us. One PIU represents one tonne of sequestrated CO_2e at a future date. The buyer can't actually say that they have offset their carbon emissions but they can say that they have demonstrated their intention to do so.

PIUs get converted, assuming the trees grow and the forest passes the Code's inspection and verification tests, into so-called Woodland Carbon Units, again with each unit representing a tonne of CO_2e. WCUs are based on actual carbon stored, using the WCC's calculation methodology.

There are other problems that the Code tries to cope with by providing safeguards. The first is the requirement of additionality – or in other words ensuring that the carbon which is being accounted for in PIUs and WCUs is 'new' carbon and not carbon which would have been stored anyway in existing woods and forests. Clearly if you've already got a forest the carbon there doesn't help solve the carbon offsetting requirement. This means for example that unfortunately the trees at Eshiels Community Woodland won't be eligible.

There are also mechanisms to cope with the fact that the additional carbon accounted for in WCUs has to be there in the long-term: if the carbon disappears into the atmosphere when the trees are cut down on maturity in, say, 35 years and is not re-sequestrated then we are clearly back to square one. So if you're signing up for accreditation under the Code you are effectively committing to very long-term forest management, even if periodically trees have to be felled and replanted.

It's little more than a decade since the Woodland Carbon Code was launched but interest has been growing very rapidly. I didn't know it as I followed the Cross Borders Drove Road from the higher ground of Minch Moor towards the valley of the Yarrow Water but there, growing slowly just alongside me as I walked down the hill, were 225 hectares of carbon units – or to be slightly more accurate 225 hectares of newly planted woodland on what had previously been rough grazing land. The trees (two-thirds Sitka, but 14% broadleaves and also some Scots

Pine) were planted in the winter of 2018-2019, and the project has been successfully validated under the WCC scheme. It's claimed that over the next 55 years over 72,000 tonnes of carbon will be captured here. 57,000 tonnes of this future carbon sequestration have already been made available for PIU purchasers.

The project which is at a place called Broadmeadows came about, I later discovered, because the local couple who owned the land and who had previously run a hill farm here were concerned at the uncertain long-term future of farming as an activity in the uplands. There were also no family members wanting ultimately to take the farm over. So their embryonic forest is designed to provide an alternative source of future income from the land they own, and while Broadmeadows is not of course a community woodland of the kind we discussed in the last chapter nevertheless there was clearly a desire by the owners to ensure that their afforestation work brought wider benefits. About a tenth of the land has been left as open ground (reportedly already being discovered by black grouse) and access routes for walkers, horse-riders and cyclists have been included.

Broadmeadows would seem to be a very effective example of carbon trading being turned to good effect. Indeed it has been highlighted by the WCC as an exemplar: "This project has given the opportunity for the landowner to diversify and remain resident as part of the local community, while realising his passion for establishing trees and maintenance of the property. The project would not have gone ahead without the prospect of additional income from carbon finance," the WCC case study advised me.

There are other examples like this in the south of Scotland. Over to the west is the inspiring example of the Borders Forest Trust, which began life more than a quarter of a century ago when a group of local people put in their own money to acquire 655 hectares of upland countryside in the Moffat Hills, on which the Trust has subsequently planted more than three-quarters of a million trees. BFT, which is a long-standing member of the Community Woodlands Association, has since gone on to acquire a further 2,500 or so hectares of land nearby where they are working to restore natural habitats and to create healthier ecosystems – or as they put it, with the aim of "reviving the wild heart of Southern Scotland".

Charles Dundas, BFT's chief executive, is quite honest that his charity's work would have to be curtailed if it were not for the opportunities which carbon trading provides. "Everything we've ever received from carbon sales has gone right into the tree planting. It's enabled the work to actually take place," he says. "Without that carbon financing element we wouldn't be able to do the work we do."

But Charles Dundas also knows that the whole idea of carbon trading is not straightforward. There are ethical qualms about it, he says: "The whole industry of carbon offsetting is currently being used as a licence to pollute. People should be reducing the need for it by reducing emissions and instead they are just buying their way out by purchasing credits."

It's a view many others have expressed. Perhaps the most eloquent critique of the whole industry is the report written by the environmental campaigner and author Alastair McIntosh. McIntosh is well known in Scotland for his pioneering work in the land reform movement, having been intimately involved in the long, high-profile and ultimately successful campaign which led to the Isle of Eigg becoming community owned in 1997 (or as he puts it, "the Isle of Eigg gaining independence from landlordism"). His forensic examination of carbon trading in Scotland which was published in the summer of 2023 bears the title *The Cheviot, the Stag and the Black, Black Carbon*, a slight re-arrangement of the title of a celebrated play by John McGrath written at the time of the North Sea oil bonanza. The arrival of carbon trading in Scotland, McIntosh suggests, is an event of similar importance to that of North Sea oil.

McIntosh has a powerful metaphor to describe carbon credits: they are, he says, the modern equivalent of mediaeval religious indulgences which people would buy to atone for their sins. Now it is carbon 'sins' which money can buy off. What's more, McIntosh adds, echoing Charles Dundas, it is by no means certain that the large companies looking to burnish their green credentials in this way have done all that they could to actually cut their emissions. Industry is in effect trading voluntary licences to enable it to carry on putting greenhouse gases into the atmosphere, he says: "At their best, they [the licences] are driven by an earnest effort at corporate social responsibility in an imperfect world where all of us who consume carbon-intensive products are responsible. At their worst, they are a calculated move by the marketing department."

Alastair McIntosh also points out that a great many trees are needed to cope with a relatively small number of emissions: a recent 240 hectare tree planting scheme in Skye will sequestrate the equivalent of the carbon produced by only forty jumbo jets flying between London and Sydney, he claims. Try to plant enough trees to sequestrate a significant amount of carbon emissions and you'd rapidly begin to gobble up the land that the world relies on to grow food.

McIntosh's main critique, however, focuses on what carbon trading is currently doing to land values and land usage in the areas being used to create carbon credits. He describes the push to acquire upland grazing land for new forestry as a Klondike rush, with British and international financial institutions leading the charge. It means, he says, that land is changing hands at prices which are likely to exclude local people wanting to move into farming.

It also means that Scotland's land is at risk of passing into ownership of institutional investors even further removed from local communities. The land, McIntosh argues, should not be "a market surface over which capital has free play": communities rather than bankers should take precedence. The danger, he adds, is community disempowerment and depopulation – history repeating itself, with this time the Clearances being for carbon rather than sheep.

It's early days in carbon trading, although those promoting it talk of likely rapid increases in the market in the years ahead (some say that PIUs which today go for perhaps £20 per unit could soon reach £60 a unit). Nevertheless prices for land do fluctuate from year to year and indeed in 2023, according to agents Strutt and Parker, upland land suitable for forestry actually went for less than in previous years. Having said that, it was still selling for around £8,600 - £10,000 a hectare which is rather a lot more than would be paid for upland grazing for a sheep farm.

And there's something else, a straw in the wind, which might suggest the way things are going. Increasingly the rhetoric from those exploiting the carbon trading market is about investing in 'natural capital'. This is a conveniently opaque term which when it was originally coined meant acknowledging the benefits and the wealth which humans draw from our lands, our geology, our soils, our water and, yes, our forests. It is posited as a third form of capital, complementing human capital and financial capital.

Doing the maths to turn stocks of sequestrated carbon into calculations which can then be monetised and traded shows just how extraordinarily inventive our financial system can be. But I don't know. I think I'd still rather call a forest a forest, rather than seeing it labelled up for sale as natural capital. And before I bought any PIUs I'd rather we worked quite a lot harder on removing our carbon emissions in the first place.

CHAPTER 6

BOWHILL

Land ownership

The first glimpse of Newark Tower comes as a surprise. A short distance south of the Yarrow Water crossing, on the lane which the Cross Borders Drove Road is following at this point, there appears through the trees the roofless but still impressive remains of a tall rectangular stone tower.

Newark Tower was originally constructed in the early fifteenth century, as one of numerous peel towers put up in Border country. They were built for a good reason. The people both north and south of the border line for many long years suffered from living in a region where the writ of central authority barely held. The writer and historian Alistair Moffat in his comprehensive account of Borders history puts it like this: "Over a huge area of mainland Britain either side of the Cheviot Hills, perhaps a tenth of the landmass of Britain, there existed a society which lived entirely beyond the laws of England and Scotland".

Moffat has also recounted the story of the Borders reivers, the gangs of cattle-thieves under the control of powerful family dynasties, who roamed these lands from the fourteenth until at least the sixteenth century. There's been a tendency in recent times to romanticise the reiver story (there's even a modern bronze statue to a 'Border Reiver', put up by a housing developer in Carlisle). But to my mind this is a story to remember but not to celebrate.

Peel towers spoke of the need for security and protection in lawless times. Newark Tower was constructed with a sizeable cellar where your cattle could be safely secured away when bands of potential cattle-thieves were in the area. The cellar later proved an all-too effective prison for hundreds of captured soldiers from the Royalist army of Charles

I, defeated at the nearby Battle of Philiphaugh in 1645 by the Scottish Covenanters' army and incarcerated in what must have been utterly inhumane conditions. (They were later to be relieved of this ordeal by being taken out and summarily executed. Those were bloody times.)

A building in the landscape like Newark Tower also communicates something else, and that is the raw power of those who control the land. It is a very physical manifestation of an economic reality which might otherwise seem much more intangible and elusive.

However nothing says 'power' quite as much as the building which is encountered just a short distance beyond Newark Tower. The imposing country mansion of Bowhill House, set in beautifully landscaped grounds complete with an ornamental loch, communicates a clear message of status, wealth and authority. A Georgian house which was much extended in the nineteenth century, Bowhill is (quoting its website for a moment) "one of the Scottish Borders' most popular visitor attractions".

Bowhill is the home of the Duke of Buccleuch, a man who has presumably learned to live with the difficulty of having a name which (if you're not Scottish or otherwise in the know) you are very likely to mispronounce. It should be *beh*CLUE, or using the phonetic spelling, bə'klu. The 'cleuch' part, more frequently spelled cleugh, is the Scots word for a steep, often wooded, valley. The word (or a variant of it) is also used in Northern English dialect.

Buccleuch has compensations enough to make up for the potential mispronunciation of his name, however. In the ranks of British aristocratic landowners the tenth Duke of Buccleuch and Queensberry, Richard Scott, more or less tops the table. As well as Bowhill, the Buccleuch estate includes the equally impressive Drumlanrig Castle in Dumfries and Galloway, which is a category A. listed castle dating back to 1691. South of the Border the Buccleuch estate also holds the equally stunning Boughton House in Northamptonshire, modestly described by its website as 'often referred to as the English Versailles'. All three of these stately homes come with substantial landholdings. There is a further 340 hectare estate at Dalkeith, just outside Edinburgh, as well as more modest land interests near Barrow-in-Furness.

Land ownership is highly significant, I would suggest, if you want to understand the landscape. In fact, I'll be deliberately provocative and put forward the assertion that, if you enjoy walking in the countryside, you'll miss half the story if you *don't* know whose land it is you are walking upon. The way that the landscape looks is extremely closely tied to the way that the land is owned.

I had entered Buccleuch lands at the moment when I'd crossed the Yarrow Water and would be staying on the Duke's lands for several further miles. Later in my walk I would be entering the estate of another Scottish landowning aristocrat, the Duke of Roxburghe. Later still as I got closer to the Border I would be on the Lothian estate, held for the Marquess of Lothian. Walking in Scotland can sometimes feel a little like a trip through Burke's Peerage.

The Buccleuch lands are (as you would anticipate) run on firm business principles, currently overseen by the Scottish banker Benny Higgins who previously ran Tesco Bank. Higgins has several separate businesses to oversee on behalf of the Duke and his family, because the Buccleuch business portfolio includes commercial forestry, agriculture, commercial and residential property and wind farm sites, as well as tourism and hospitality businesses. The three big houses Bowhill, Drumlanrig and Boughton are all open as visitor attractions.

Buccleuch occupies a position in the heart of the Scottish, and British, establishment and the current Duke had his education at Eton and Christ Church, Oxford, before inheriting his title on the death of his father. His dynasty goes back to the first of Charles II's illegitimate children, the Duke of Monmouth, who was born to one of Charles's lovers when he was in exile in the Netherlands shortly after his father Charles I's execution in 1649. The Scott family tree however goes back far beyond the creation of the Dukedom, to at least the thirteenth century. Auld blood.

For many years the Duke of Buccleuch's landholdings meant that his was the name at the top of the table of private landowners in Scotland, and in second place in the overall list of all Scottish landowners (behind the forestry and agricultural lands held in public ownership). This was an exposed position to occupy and certainly meant that Buccleuch came in for what was sometimes unwelcome publicity when land ownership matters were being discussed. Perhaps to remedy this, or perhaps simply to rebalance the investment portfolio, the Buccleuch estate has recently sold off about a third of its holdings. It is now simply the second largest private landowner and the fourth overall landowner in Scotland, with about 65,000 hectares.

To be fair the Buccleuch estate has in recent times tried to meet some of the previous criticism it faced by being much more transparent about the extent of its holdings. Comprehensive maps of these are now openly available online on its website.

But in any case we need to broaden this beyond one individual and his land: I don't want to personalise this around the Duke of Buccleuch. It is simply conveniently fortuitous for my narrative that at this point in my story the Cross Borders Drove Road I was following passed close to Bowhill – so close indeed that on my walk I may inadvertently have trespassed into that part of Bowhill's ornamental parkland that you're supposed to pay to visit, since the footpath signposts at this point rather let me down. (Memo to Bowhill Estate Manager: get someone out to check the waymarks on the paths at the back of the loch.)

We need to look at the bigger picture. Land ownership and land reform has been high on the political agenda of the post-devolution Scottish Parliament in the years since 1999 in a way that it hasn't been in England. South of the border, what used to be known as the 'land question' hasn't really been a pressing issue in Parliament for a century, not since the time when Lloyd George tried to introduce a measure of land value taxation in his so-called People's Budget of 1909 and the House of Lords promptly said no and precipitated a constitutional crisis. It's hard to recall now that in the early years of the twentieth century land was such a dominant political concern, or to remember for example that the Land Nationalisation Society was a powerful pressure group with the ear of some of the leading politicians of the day.

By contrast to England, the Scottish Parliament has passed two Land Reform Acts since 1999 and was discussing a third as this book was prepared for publication. We have seen (page 9) how the first Land Reform Act of 2003 established the presumption of open access to Scotland's countryside but that Act also strengthened crofting rights and introduced a potential community right to buy for land in rural areas. The latter provisions were strengthened a little by the Community Empowerment Act of 2015 which, let me remind you, helped the Peebles Community Trust acquire Eshiels Wood. A year later in 2016 came Scotland's second Land Reform Act which among other things established a Scottish Land Commission charged with preparing a more strategic approach to Scottish land issues.

One reason why land has featured so strongly in Scottish political discourse is that the country has probably the most concentrated pattern of land ownership in Europe. The market in land is also effectively unregulated, so that there are currently no restrictions on who can acquire land when it comes on the market. At the moment all sorts of people can and do acquire Scotland's mountains and glens. The Buccleuch family dynasty may be Scottish through-and-through but there are estates in Scotland owned by individuals from all around the world, quite often setting things up so that ownership is formally held in tax havens in places like the Cayman Islands. In fact, 71 offshore companies between them currently own 262,489 hectares of Scotland.

The community buyout of the land of the Isle of Eigg by Alastair McIntosh and his colleagues (page 41) was brought about as a response to the fact that the previous owner, who was German, had allowed the island's infrastructure to crumble and its economy to wither away. An earlier successful community buy-out in 1993 of the North Lochinver estate in Sutherland prised the estate away from the hands of a company which had gone bust, this time a concern legally based in Sweden. There have been other heartening stories of local communities managing to acquire the lands they live on, sometimes from overseas owners but often from Scottish owners wanting to sell. They include high-profile initiatives in Knoydart, North Harris and South Uist as well as the example of the North West Mull and Ulva buy-out already mentioned (page 25).

These examples are in the Highlands and Islands, but the most recent significant community land acquisition by contrast was in the southern uplands, in the lands around the town of Langholm where the vendor was none other than the Buccleuch estate, the sale being part of its portfolio rebalancing exercise. The community-led Langholm Initiative successfully raised the £6m required to acquire over 4,200 hectares of land, much of it previously grouse moorland, which has now become the Tarras Valley Nature Reserve. Initiatives like this demonstrate that there can be different ways of holding land, ways which can benefit both the environment and the people who live on it or want to visit it. These alternative models can be prefigurative of a future that is organised in a different, better, way.

But we should perhaps not get carried away. Despite all the hard work by people in many Scottish communities in recent decades and despite the efforts of the Land Reform legislation of the Scottish Parliament, less than 3% of Scotland's land is held in some form of community-owned tenure. By contrast, 83% of Scotland remains privately owned.

It would take a utopian leap of faith to imagine that these percentages could be reversed any time soon or that a UK or Scottish government would ever move to expropriate the land from its current owners. Buying private land to any extent with public money is also unrealistic: there are not the public resources available to do more than scratch the surface. The Scottish Land Fund, as we've seen (page 26), currently caps its maximum contribution to £1m. Anyway, the question has to be posed as to whether it is really the best use of public funds to simply put money into the hands of private individuals.

What's a Scottish mountain or island really worth, in any case? Buying a Scottish estate is more often than not a vanity project for the super-rich. To quote the words of one market report, it is "a luxury purchase to enjoy, not unlike a superyacht or a Lamborghini". This means that prices paid are likely to bear little or no relationship to the actual economic potential of the underlying land. Land prices are decided on the open market and by market forces alone. And successful purchasers, at least for the present, need to have little or no regard for the social and economic consequences of their actions.

This was an issue acknowledged by the Rural Affairs Minister Mairi Gougeon when she presented the latest Land Reform measures to the Scottish Parliament in 2024: "Too often people and communities feel powerless when the land they live on is sold with no prior warning," she said. "We do not think it is right that ownership and control of much of Scotland's land is still in the hands of relatively few people." The measures she was proposing certainly proved unpopular with the landowners' body Scottish Land and Estates which described the government as in thrall to "outdated ideology" and engaging in a "destructive and disproportionate attack" on landed estates. (This is admittedly slightly more restrained language than that used by one right-of-centre newspaper at the time of the 2003 Land Reform Act which described the reforms as "inspired by class hatred" and designed to turn Scotland into the "Albania of northern Europe".)

However, there are also those who see the latest attempt at land reform as little more than bureaucratic tinkering with the underlying problems. The measures aim to intervene to mitigate the workings of the market, but recommendations from the Scottish Land Commission to introduce tighter restrictions on who can own land and for a public interest test to be required when land changes hands are not currently expected to be in the eventual legislation.

One of those less than convinced that the latest land reform legislation will achieve much is the individual who more than any other single person has looked in detail at land ownership issues in Scotland. Andy Wightman is the author of the pioneering 1996 book *Who Owns Scotland* and of the extended sequel *The Poor Had no Lawyer: Who owns Scotland (and how they got it)*, which first came out in 2010 and which has now gone into several revised editions. His recent briefing note *Who Owns Scotland 2024* is the source of the data on Scottish land ownership which I have used earlier in this chapter.

After my walk was over and when I was working on this chapter I contacted Andy Wightman and he generously agreed to share with me some of his thoughts. After a short period recently spent as an MSP (and a shorter time as a Minister in the SNP/Green coalition government), he has left politics behind and is once again working as an independent researcher and writer. His website whoownsscotland. org.uk is a remarkable achievement, providing the sort of detail on individual land ownership which should have been made available years ago by government, but wasn't. I was happy to make the very modest subscription necessary to find out for myself whose land I was tramping over as I made my journey south.

For Andy Wightman, one problem which needs addressing is the issue of inflated land values. "One of the key things we need to do is to get land values down to nearer the economic value rather than the speculative value of the land," he told me. Estates are going for several million pounds when the income that the underlying land could generate is barely a fraction of this. "If you restricted ownership in some way, if for example you imposed residency conditions, that would immediately reduce the pool of people willing to buy, and they would pay less for it because they wouldn't be competing with Arab sheiks or whoever," Wightman added.

And then there is the question of taxation. "Tax is a really important topic. The baker and hairdresser in a small town in Galloway are paying non-domestic rates but a multi-million pound farming business just outside the village is paying nothing," Wightman went on. Landholdings are outside the business rates system and also benefit from various kinds of Inheritance Tax and Capital Gains Tax relief. The question perhaps to consider is whether these tax reliefs are still appropriate and whether they contribute to, or detract from, the sorts of public policies which our governments are attempting to work towards.

Does it really matter so very much, though, if land ownership remains concentrated in the hands of a few lucky people? Are we simply allowing ourselves to give vent to that 'class hatred' which the newspaper back in 2003 claimed to have identified? What harm really is there if some people who can afford it choose to invest in land, rather than spending their wealth in some other way?

Those who are active in land reform circles in Scotland would reply that yes, it matters, because the current arrangements do cause harm. There is significant evidence, they would argue, that land ownership patterns cause damage to rural economies, to local communities and to local culture. But they would go further and would also claim to have proof that the way the land is owned is causing environmental degradation and loss of biodiversity. The finger is particularly pointed at the current use of the big landed estates for shooting, the corollary to which is that large areas of countryside have become occupied by very great numbers of deer which are not subject to natural predation and which are causing damage to natural woodland regeneration. Too many glens have too many 'monarchs', you might say: the argument is that deer numbers have to be brought down.

So if we are serious in wanting to address climate change and biodiversity loss we can't afford not to look at issues of land ownership, I was told. I am minded to give the last word to Andy Wightman: "There should be a duty which comes with ownership of land," he said. "It's about responsibilities, and particularly the responsibility to steward nature. Ultimately if you own land, that's your duty, that's your job".

CHAPTER 7

CARTERHAUGH

Tam Lin

There are no interpretation boards in place at Carterhaugh, and certainly no souvenir shops. There's really nothing at all to suggest that anyone might want to come here as a tourist or indeed for any reason other than to visit the people living in the substantial house up the drive which hides behind a 'Private' sign.

But I was prepared to make a diversion from the route which I could have followed from Bowhill. Carterhaugh, I decided, had to be on my itinerary.

When I'd mentioned this beforehand to friends the vast majority had looked blank. 'Tam Lin', I'd said encouragingly. They still shrugged. Just a handful nodded back in recognition. "Carterhaugh is an actual place?" said one friend. "I always thought it must be a made-up name."

I should explain. Tam Lin is a ballad, one of what are sometimes called Scottish and English traditional ballads, or popular ballads, or – rather inaccurately – Border ballads (because they were certainly not just sung in the Borders). And Carterhaugh, it has to be said, is the one place you're instructed *not* to visit in the first verse of the ballad.

Or at least, this is the way that the version of Tam Lin which was collected by Robert Burns starts. Burns' interest in traditional song is well-known and was to be a strong influence in his own writings, and he was responsible for passing on the text to the Scottish music engraver James Johnson, for the 1792 volume of Johnson's multi-part collection of old Scottish songs called, slightly curiously, *The Scots Musical Museum*. Indeed, without Burns on hand to feed him material, Johnson might have floundered: around a third of the six hundred ballads he included in his books came from Burns.

There is no 'correct' version of Tam Lin. Francis James Child, the American scholar who published in the late nineteenth century his authoritative *The English and Scottish Popular Ballads* included nine versions of Tam Lin, one of which is Burns' version and another of which had in fact been collected by Walter Scott. Scott published this in another now equally famous early anthology of Scottish traditional ballads, his *Minstrelsy of the Scottish Border*.

As it happens, both Burns' and Scott's versions start the ballad the same way, and this is, too, the first verse which is likely to be familiar to most people today – most people, that is, who know Tam Lin at all, because it appears rather regrettably as though this part of our common cultural heritage is now beginning to disappear. If you do know Tam Lin, it may well be because you know the version the folk-rock band Fairport Convention included in their 1969 album *Liege and Lief*, where the vocals are sung by Sandy Denny over a driving guitar line insistently pushing the song forward. Certainly *Liege and Lief* was my own introduction to Tam Lin, although the song has also been recorded by several other artists. Much more recently, as part of The Imagined Village folk project, there was a fascinating if tangential tribute paid to the ballad in *Tam Lyn Retold*, featuring poet Benjamin Zephaniah.

Among other things the contents of the Tam Lin ballad offers youthful rebellion, forbidden sex resulting in pregnancy, a midnight encounter at Halloween, magic, shape-shifting, and a risky, touch-and-go escape from fairy captivity at the end for one of the main characters, Tam Lin himself. Soap operas today could hardly do any better. Here's how the first verse gets us started:

> *O I forbid you, maidens a',*
> *That wear gowd in your hair,*
> *To come and gae by Carterhaugh,*
> *For young Tam Lin is there.*

In the way that is familiar in many of the traditional ballads, no time is wasted at the start with unnecessary scene-setting. There is no introduction, and no explanation either as to who is speaking, simply their warning words.

I can imagine a cheap paperback you pick up in an airport starting in a similar way:

> *Absolutely not, he said, almost shouting at me. "I completely*
> *forbid it." I saw his face contort with anger. "Let me make myself*

> *clear. You're never ever to go to Carterhaugh." I shrugged. "Don't*
> *look at me like that," he went on. "You know very well who's at*
> *Carterhaugh. Young Tam Lin is there."*

I'd like to think that, after that opening paragraph, you might carry on reading my novel.

The ballad is now known universally as Tam Lin, but the major protagonist in it is a young woman called Janet (she is Margaret or Jennet in some versions, but let's stick with Janet). Janet rapidly demonstrates that she has no inclination to obey any male diktat. As soon as verse three we gather that:

> *Janet has kilted her green kirtle*
> *A little aboon her knee*
> *And she has broded her yellow hair*
> *A little above her bree,*
> *And she's awa to Carterhaugh*
> *As fast as she can hie.*

So much for patriarchal strictures about young women's activities.

Janet demonstrates herself equally feisty when, predictably, she meets Tam Lin at Carterhaugh and, less predictably, he tells her off for coming there without *his* permission. The reply comes:

> *I'll come and gang by Carterhaugh*
> *And ask nae leave at thee*

Go, Janet! Anyway, after this initial verbal tussle things appear to go rather better between Janet and Tam Lin because almost the next thing we know is that Janet is pregnant.

Things now take an unexpected turn as it becomes apparent that Tam Lin is not just a rather dishy young man but has something of the supernatural about him. Janet's forthcoming child, it seems, may have been fathered not by a human but by an elfin knight. Naturally somewhat concerned at the implications of this, Janet ponders her options (some versions have her looking for a herb which might be able to bring on an abortion). She meets Tam Lin again who, telling her not to harm the unborn baby, reveals his story to her. Yes, he was once a human knight, properly christened and all that, but one unfortunate day he had taken a fall from his horse and that had enabled him to be captured by the Queen of the Fairies "in yon green hill to dwell".

There is however a slim chance, just one opportunity, for Janet to break the magic spell he is under and get her lover back.

Conveniently, it is Halloween, when the fairies will be out riding, and Tam Lin will be among them.

> *Just at the mirk and midnight hour*
> *The fairy folk will ride*
> *And they that wad their true-love win*
> *At Miles Cross they maun bide.*

So Janet heads to Miles Cross and hides herself there in the dark. Tam Lin will be riding a 'milk-white steed', he tells her, and when she sees the horse her task is to run forward as quickly as she can and pull him off. She is forewarned that fairy magic will then be employed. Tam Lin will be shape-shifted into all sorts of unpleasant things: a newt, an adder, a bear, a lion, a red-hot iron, a burning fire, until finally he is turned into a naked man. Tam Lin gives her instructions:

> *But hold me fast and fear me not*
> *I am your bairn's father.*

Janet does as she has been advised and holds on tight. Tam Lin is safely returned from the fairy to the human kingdom. The Queen of the Fairies, the end of the ballad informs us, is furious: Janet has taken away her bonniest knight.

As for the lovers we are told nothing more. Let us assume they live happily ever after, baby and all.

It has to be said, nevertheless, that a happy ending is not precisely the norm among the 305 traditional ballads that Child included in his collection: much more often the breaking of social taboos (as for example sexual liaison outside marriage) ends up being punished, often with gory deaths of the lovers. This is certainly what happens at the end of the other traditional ballad which Fairport Convention included on their *Liege and Lief* album, the one where Lady Darnell goes to church one New Year, spots Matty Groves in the crowd and propositions him, only for Lord Darnell to return unexpectedly that evening to find the two lovers in flagrante.

So it is unusually refreshing that in Tam Lin Janet's defiance of accepted social behaviour ultimately brings her reward rather than punishment.

The strong female character of Janet is unusual, too, and has meant that the Tam Lin ballad has attracted particular attention. Several feminist authors have in recent years adapted the story into prose, particularly in illustrated books and stories aimed at children and young adults. There has also been considerable academic work focused on the ballad. The US professor Martha Hixon, for example, wrote an influential paper back in 2004 with the title *Tam Lin, Fair Janet and the Sexual Revolution*. As she points out, "Though the ballad is named after the kidnapped knight, Tam Lin, the hero of the tale is actually Janet... That it is a female who saves the man in this story both makes the tale an interesting inversion of the traditional male hero motif and establishes a particular relevancy for modern readers".

One of the areas which she and other writers have explored is the extent to which the popular ballad tradition was one associated more with women rather than men. Certainly Francis James Child believed that women were a more fertile source of material than were men. Several of the ballads which ended up in his anthology were collected originally from a woman called Anna Gordon who was born in Aberdeen in 1747 and who, although coming from a middle-class milieu, learned the ballads she remembered from her mother, from an aunt and from a female servant. "As far as they can be traced, then, Anna Gordon's ballads are stories of a woman's tradition; her three immediate sources were women," was the observation of the Scottish author and folklorist David Buchan in his celebrated book *The Ballad and the Folk*. It's true that men sang the traditional ballads, but perhaps women sang them more frequently – and perhaps for this reason many of the ballads deal with issues of personal relationships, of women's control (or lack of control) over their lives and particularly over their fertility, and of attempts to find ways that this lack of control might be circumvented.

Tam Lin is, as I've said, a 'traditional' ballad but what precisely does 'traditional' mean? No-one can say quite how early some of these ballads first began to be sung and passed on from one singer to another, but undoubtedly they have been a part of shared culture for centuries. In Britain it's certainly fair to say that the ballads were a living part of popular culture during the seventeenth, eighteenth and nineteenth centuries, but even in the twentieth century (many long years after the first collectors believed they were recording a dying tradition) more recent folk song collectors were transcribing ballads from traditional singers who learned them from other singers. Child reported that the first reference to the 'Tayl of the young Tamlene' that he could trace was to a book published in 1549 and he also found another mention of the story just a few years after that. But as he pointed out, elements of the story (including for example the way that Tam Lin is shape-shifted by magic into wild animals) are to be found in myths and legends in other European countries going right back to earliest times.

So perhaps this is the moment to consider the historical place of fairy-folk in the context of the Scottish landscape – the cultural landscape, that is, because I would not want to be challenged for making assertions about their place in the physical landscape.

We are (of course we are) these days a rationally minded people who have put superstitious beliefs behind us and can dismiss talk of fairies as – well – simply fairy tales. Those tiny creatures with their gossamer wings are today fit just for picture books to entertain our little ones, before our children grow up and put away childish things. Some people in the past may have thought differently but maybe people in the past were simply a lot more gullible than we are today. And if there are people who still today would claim to believe in super-natural phenomena of this sort of magical kind, well, such beliefs are no doubt harmless enough. We can smile knowingly when, for example, news stories appear of road construction projects in Iceland having to be halted because of fears that that the huldufólk, the hidden folk or elves, would otherwise be disturbed.

But fairies or elves were undoubtedly part of the daily lives of people in our island too in times past. "That many people in pre-industrial Europe believed in fairies cannot be disputed on the basis of the available evidence. They were a part of everyday life, as real to people as the sunrise." So write Lizanne Henderson and Edward J. Cowan in their book *Scottish Fairy Belief.* In terms of Scotland itself, they add: "By the eve of Reformation the fairies were well and truly established in Scotland, acknowledged, accepted and best avoided by people at all levels of society who apparently took them quite seriously, save for a small group of intellectuals who hovered in court circles".

I confess to heading in this direction at this point in this chapter somewhat apprehensively, in case you should begin to have doubts as to my reliability as a travel companion. Indeed after I had ordered a copy of *Scottish Fairy Belief* I wondered whether this was a book that needed hiding away, in case friends saw it and began to be concerned for me. I need not have worried about the book, of course. Lizanne Henderson and Edward Cowan approach the subject from impeccable academic backgrounds (Cowan before his death in 2022 was Professor of Scottish History at the University of Glasgow) and, as they explain in their introduction, they are most definitely not trying to prove the reality or otherwise of fairies ("such an endeavour would be as futile as it is irrelevant"). What they *do* seek to explore is the nature of the beliefs that people held, because "what we can prove is that many Scots people, who lived mainly in the period from c 1450 to c 1750, had no doubt that fairies actually existed". In other words, theirs is a study to be filed under social history or social anthropology.

What actually comes to light is a belief system in a whole galaxy of supernatural spirits, including for example the humble brownies who chose to live in households where they helped out by undertaking domestic chores. (Ah, what a shame brownies seem not to be with us these days.) Rev. Robert Kirk, the minister at Aberfoyle who wrote a manuscript entitled *The Secret Common-Wealth of Elves, Fauns and Fairies* in the late seventeenth century, felt that fairy beings were everywhere, "as thick as atomes in the air". Part of God's creation, they moved among humans but were only very occasionally to be glimpsed or interacted with.

Elves and fairies appear to have been synonymous terms in Scotland (the Northern Isles had trows or trolls, a reflection of the strong Scandinavian tradition there), but there were also all sorts of euphemisms. Henderson and Cowan offer a list: the good folk, the good neighbours, the gentry, the hill folk, the honest folk, and many more. A euphemism could be very necessary as a way of avoiding having to spell out exactly what you were talking about, because it also seems clear that it was best not to meddle in fairy business. Fairies could be dangerous neighbours, and if at all possible it was good policy to placate them.

Fairies may have been as thick as atomes, but there were places where they could particularly be found to congregate – green hills or fairy glens, for example. It was as though there were a separate supernatural landscape which overlay our own natural landscape like a thin film. And there were times when the boundary between these worlds could be crossed, as Tam Lin discovered when he fell from his horse and as Janet discovered too as she wrenched Tam Lin back to the human world.

The key word here is liminal, meaning a threshold. Henderson and Cowan put it like this: "The fairies themselves were liminal creatures...

Elfland existed in other-space, a place that was so near and yet so far. It was, in many ways, an inversion of the human world, with its own laws, but unlike Heaven and Hell, Fairyland existed on earth."

I realised belatedly that I had walked very close to what many people in times past had regarded as a liminal threshold when I was on the Cross Borders Drove Road on Minch Moor. I will call on Walter Scott to explain: "There is, upon the top of Minchmuir, a mountain in Peebles-shire, a spring, called the Cheese Well, because, anciently, those who passed that way were wont to throw into it a piece of cheese, as an offering to the Fairies, to whom it was consecrated". There is indeed something very magical about coming across the Cheese Well, a source of spring water high up on land which is otherwise dry. The water the day I passed by was rather dirty and uninviting but as the day was as hot as ever and as the water in my water bottles was running low, I stooped down to dip my cap into the well and let it splash over my head. A moment to cool off. I had no cheese with me to proffer in exchange for the water, but I did say a silent thank you to the spring. And of course to whoever else might have been there, across the threshold, watching my passing.

The idea of liminal places remains today in the world of fiction. I'm thinking for example of Philip Pullman's popular trilogy *His Dark Materials*, in which the two central characters Lyra Belacqua and Will Parry do indeed find themselves moving between parallel universes as the plot unfolds. For that matter the idea of multiple worlds, or the multiverse, is a hypothesis that some physicists put forward in all seriousness as a potential way of interpreting reality. Just saying…

The day which had brought me to Carterhaugh had started pretty early, when I'd folded away the tent and munched for breakfast a rather stale croissant I'd bought the night before in Peebles. It had been a long, hot day since then and I suppose I could have been disappointed to find that Carterhaugh was in the end simply just another fairly substantial house in the Borders. But actually I think I was relieved not to be greeted by any tourist busyness there. A van parked in the driveway suggested that I'd come on a day when the house owners were having their TV aerial adjusted. Everyday life. Nothing very magical.

I slipped away, respecting the 'Private' sign. But before I resumed my walk down to the Ettrick Water and then onwards towards Selkirk I walked just a few yards further along the country road beyond Carterhaugh. My map had suggested that somewhere hereabouts was something I should check out. It took a little perseverance to find it, but indeed there it was: a small stone rectangle beside a wall, filled with very dirty water seeping out of the field above. A sign alongside, a relatively modern one, told me I had found what I was looking for. Tamlane Well, it read.

He's not entirely forgotten hereabouts.

CHAPTER 8

SELKIRK

Rivers, floods

The rivers of the Scottish Borders were there as a form of punctuation to mark my progress south from Edinburgh. First was the Tweed at Peebles. After Minch Moor came Yarrow Water. Shortly after I'd left Carterhaugh a rather overgrown riverside footpath took me to a small pedestrian bridge where I met Ettrick Water. Later (two days later in fact) the Teviot would be waiting for me.

Yarrow Water is swallowed up by Ettrick Water only a little distance from Carterhaugh and the newly enlarged waters of the Ettrick are in turn taken over by the river Tweed a little way downstream from Selkirk. Later, even further downstream at Kelso, the Teviot meets the same fate. By the time the Tweed reaches England and the North Sea at Berwick its waters will have drained some 4,000 square kilometres of Scottish border countryside.

The Tweed basin is special of course. This is the place to come if you want to try your hand (and test your bank account) at fly fishing for salmon. The task of protecting the fishing, ensuring that the salmon can safely migrate upstream to spawn, and watching out for anyone tempted to do some illicit poaching is in the hands of the River Tweed Commission, a body that goes back 200 years and is made up of local councillors, anglers and representatives of the local businesses there to provide for the needs of fishermen. The Commission also polices the North Sea's inshore waters down to Lindisfarne and northwards from Berwick to beyond St Abb's Head.

The Tweed basin has maximum conservation protection. Its waters (including the Yarrow, Ettrick and Teviot tributaries as far back as their sources) have been declared a Special Area of Conservation (SAC), a designation originally established under the European Union's 1992 Habitats Directive but which has survived Brexit and is now under the auspices of the UK-wide Joint Nature Conservation Committee. SAC designation is given to those parts of our countryside, water as well as land, which are felt to be of the highest importance in conservation terms.

The Tweed basin shares its SAC status with a second designation, as a Site of Special Scientific Interest. SSSIs go back further than SACs, having been introduced in the landmark National Parks and Access to the Countryside Act of 1949. In total there are over a hundred SSSIs across the UK, with around half of them protecting rivers and their waters.

Why is the Tweed basin an SAC and a SSSI? As you might imagine, it's much to do with the Atlantic salmon. Salmon need good quality water and the Tweed and its tributaries can provide it. There is a strong run of salmon each Autumn and another, smaller, run of the fish each Spring. Salmon share the rivers with the lamprey, another species of fish which is important in conservation terms and which also comes this way to spawn. More accurately, the Tweed basin is home to three species of this fish, the sea lamprey, river lamprey and the brook lamprey.

It is not just the fly-fishermen who pose a challenge to these fish as they make their way up- and downstream. The SAC and SSSI designations also note the importance of these rivers for otters, a mammal which is certainly partial to a salmon or lamprey although it will also be happy if eels, trout or frogs come its way. Keeping the river water clear and unpolluted is important to maintain the otter populations too.

Fish, mammals, and also invertebrates: over half of all the mayfly species found in Britain can be found in the Tweed basin, a quarter of all our caddisfly species and, oh, stoneflies, soldier flies, dance flies, craneflies and more. I could go on. I think you are getting the message.

When it comes to the landscape, therefore, these Scottish Borders rivers are highly significant features. Once upon a time they would have presented challenges to travellers, who would have had to make long diversions or look for safe fords. Fortunately we now have bridges. Indeed if you're in a car you may not even notice the rivers as you hurry past. But particularly in recent years the Tweed and its tributaries have been making it clear that they are not to be taken for granted.

Flooding has been a problem historically for the settlements along the river banks. I wasn't there myself but I'm told that 1767 was a problem year. March 1881 saw extensive flooding on the Tweed, Ettrick Water and Teviot. Galashiels had its worst floods for 36 years in 1927. Peebles suffered in 1937. The railway line between Melrose and Newtown St Boswells was washed away in 1948. There was further flooding in different parts of the Tweed basin in, for example, October 1949 and January 1951 and August 1956 and January 1962 and October 1977. Galashiels copped it again in 1984.

But the years since the start of the twenty-first century have seen flooding become much more prevalent. Peebles for example suffered from floods caused by Storm Frank in December 2015 when homes and a nursing home were flooded, and again from Storm Ciara in February 2020. Hawick, on the Teviot, has had flooding in October 2002, January 2005, October 2005, December 2013, twice over the winter of 2015/16 and again much more recently (there are dramatic videos of the 2021 flooding in Hawick still up on YouTube).

Ettrick Water and Yarrow Water also caused major problems in Selkirk in the early years of this century. A particularly bad flood took place in May 2003 when flooding affected over 150 homes and badly damaged bridges over the Ettrick. There were floods a year later, in August 2004, and again in November 2012. Businesses in the Riverside Business Park estate, which houses one of the most important employment areas in the Scottish Borders, have been affected by flooding (their owners may perhaps have wondered afterwards if they should have thought a little more carefully about the implication of the name of their estate).

Recent serious flooding has not been a feature just in the Tweed basin, of course. It has been a phenomenon in cities and towns across the UK. Those organisations engaged in the task of sorting out the problem – the Environment Agency in England and the Scottish Environment Protection Agency, SEPA, in Scotland – have had to tear up earlier predictions of the statistical probability of flooding events. The finger is pointed firmly at the effects of climate change.

"Anyone who has been in a flood area knows the intimidating terror it can bring. The foreboding that comes as people confront the potential damage or destruction of homes, businesses and other properties as well as injuries and, in the worst cases, loss of life. This is all being made worse by the Climate Emergency," wrote SEPA's Chief Executive in 2021 in his introduction to his organisation's flood risk management plans. SEPA has estimated that there are currently 284,000 homes and businesses in Scotland at risk of flooding but it says that the climate emergency potentially will bring in a further 110,000 homes and businesses if steps are not taken to try to reduce the risks.

So serious public money is being spent to try to do just this. Selkirk was one of the first towns in the Tweed basin to have a flood alleviation scheme undertaken, with work starting in 2014 and finishing in 2017. The project included more than 3km of flood walls and a further 3km of embankments as well as work on several bridges across the Ettrick Water, including a major new three-span steel bridge. All these works cost in total just under £32m but most local people say that the money has been well spent. Potentially serious flooding was avoided in 2015 (when the works were only partly complete), in 2017 and again in 2020. Those businesses in the Riverside estate can breathe a sigh of relief.

More recently a similar scheme has been under way further south for the town of Hawick, where the need has if anything been even greater than in Selkirk. The cost for Hawick is estimated at £91m, although this admittedly includes additional benefits for the town including a new cycleway.

Despite the big money, generally alleviation works like these satisfactorily pass benefit-cost scrutiny. As well as all the human costs, flooding has a significant financial cost: SEPA says that the cost of flooding in the Tweed basin area, averaged out year-on-year, works out at around £11.6m per year.

We are, you might say, paying the cost of years of inaction. For many years, we allowed houses (business parks, too) to be built too close to our rivers. We failed to remember that flood plains were there for a purpose. We forgot our history and became blasé about the possibility of flooding returning in the future. But also we allowed those greenhouse gas emissions to continue to be pumped into the atmosphere, pushing up temperatures and increasing the risk of severe weather events. Now, at something like the last minute, we are preparing the necessary flood risk management strategies and calling in the construction contractors with the heavy plant to try to protect us. Prevention would have been better than cure but we're left hoping that the cures we are putting in place will do the trick.

Having said that, the Ettrick Water was on its very best behaviour as I walked the last few miles along its south bank towards the centre of Selkirk. My campsite was beside the Leisure Centre, down the hill from the historic heart of the burgh, in the extensive park which borders Ettrick Water. I slept peacefully, safe and sound… and dry.

Leaving Selkirk early the next morning involved clambering up to the town centre and then carrying on to the slopes of the old common land known as Selkirk Hill. "Look out for the orchids," a dog-walker who passed me called across and we stopped and chatted. Indeed Selkirk Hill is attractive countryside, with several species of orchids growing at different times of the year among the grasses and with a wide range of bird life too. I had said goodbye to the Cross Borders Drove Road for the last time the previous afternoon just before Selkirk and I was now following another long-distance trail, the Borders Abbeys Way. It was pleasant walking. My route, just for the time being, was no longer southerly, but rather northwards or at least north-eastwards. Melrose was the immediate destination.

CHAPTER 9

MELROSE

Waiting for the train

I gave myself time to explore Melrose. Of all the Border burghs Melrose is the one which tends to be first on visitors' lists. The big draw is Melrose Abbey, the ruins of which dominate the eastern end of the town. Most of the great Abbey church has been open to the skies above for centuries but what's still there remains by any measure extremely impressive.

There was a very early community of Christian monks in Melrose, or at least a little way to the east in what is now called Old Melrose. St Cuthbert, the seventh century ascetic who many claim as the patron saint of Northumberland, came from the Borders area and joined the monastery as a young man after apparently experiencing a vision on the night that St Aidan, the founder of Lindisfarne, died. Cuthbert, a significant figure in early British Christianity whose life was later to be written up by the Venerable Bede, was Prior of the monastery at Old Melrose for a number of years before later being appointed Bishop of Lindisfarne. He ended his life living the existence of a hermit, having retreated from the world to a cell on one of the Inner Farne islands.

But Melrose Abbey was not the monastery Cuthbert knew, which seems to have survived only until around the ninth century. A new Christian monastic community, a Cistercian one, was established in the twelfth century in the lands two miles or so further west and it was around this monastery that the present town of Melrose developed. The monks came here at the behest of the then King of Scotland David I, David being also responsible for the establishment of several of the other famous abbeys and religious houses of the Scottish Borders including those at Jedburgh and Kelso.

However what we see today at Melrose Abbey isn't that twelfth century foundation either but rather the result of the rebuilding of the Abbey and its grounds in the late fourteenth and fifteenth centuries. An English army led by King Richard II had invaded the Border lands in 1385 and while they were visiting they decided to take the opportunity to plunder and destroy the original Cistercian buildings.

The Cistercian monks were a contemplative order but on the other hand Melrose Abbey was by the 1380s a powerful economic presence in the region, and one that therefore could exercise political influence. The Cistercians had acquired much land, at least ten thousand hectares by this stage, and were using their land to develop a major sheep-rearing and wool exporting business operation. One of their granges, or sheep farms, was just up the hill from Melrose at Eildon and the monks also had lands much more widely spread across the Borders. As we've seen (page 33) Tom Devine described the eighteenth-century Borders Clearances as being characterised by a seemingly inexorable white tide of sheep being introduced for large-scale farming but in many ways the landowners then were merely replicating what the monks had been doing many centuries earlier.

So Richard II might have simply been feeling vindictive when he ordered the destruction of Melrose Abbey but it's possible that he may have been trying to attack the temporal as opposed to the spiritual power that the Abbey exercised at the time. The Abbey, once rebuilt, was to suffer further damage again from English armies in the mid-sixteenth century and the last Abbot at Melrose died in 1557. Later on, some of the ruined Abbey church was for a time converted into a parish church for Melrose.

The Melrose area has other draws for visitors, particularly Abbotsford a few miles west. Abbotsford, the home of Sir Walter Scott, was originally a simple farmhouse but was converted by Scott into a rambling and whimsical country house – the term which springs to mind to describe it is 'country pile'. Scott bought what had previously been known locally as Clarty Hole in 1811, renaming it in tribute to the nearby ford across the Tweed which he claimed had been used by the Melrose Abbey monks.

As a writer Scott has rather fallen out of favour these days and his novels are more often to be bought in fancy bindings from antiquarian booksellers than found on the shelves of mainstream bookshops. But Scott's role in reinterpreting Scottish history and in establishing the image of the country which still brings in the foreign tourists today was a seminal one. It's not an accident that the publicity material for Abbotsford, after a necessary nod to Scott's novels, goes on to describe him as the man who "popularised tartan, saved the Scottish banknote and rediscovered his country's Crown Jewels".

Abbotsford's extensive parkland and grounds have been formally declared to be a designated landscape by Historic Environment Scotland and the house itself has the highest category of architectural listing in Scotland, Category A., being described as "one of the most important nineteenth century buildings in Scotland". Abbotsford in fact effectively marked the beginning of the Scottish Baronial Revival movement, the deliberate desire to replicate traditional Scottish castle architecture.

Melrose has another building which has been seen fit to be awarded Category A. listing for its architectural significance and it is not what you might immediately expect. It is Melrose's railway station.

The railway arrived in Melrose in 1849, initially on the line between Edinburgh and Hawick. This was later extended in 1862 to Carlisle to create a main line railway which became known (in tribute to Walter Scott and his Waverley novels) as the 'Waverley Route'. Perhaps also as a nod to the memory of Scott (who had died at Abbotsford in 1832) Melrose station was designed to be a powerful architectural statement in its own right. It is 'Jacobean' in style, or in other words it was designed to look like a country mansion copying traditional Jacobean style, with a full set of elaborately constructed chimneys, mullioned windows, ornamental finials and the like. On the platform side great iron and timber canopies were erected, one of which remains today looking a little like a cut-down racecourse pavilion or football stand. Melrose station was described when it opened as the handsomest provincial station in the country and its Category A. classification confirms that it remains of continuing significance as an exemplar of the golden years of railway architecture.

What Melrose station does *not* have today, however, are any trains. The Waverley Route north from Carlisle to Edinburgh was controversially closed in January 1969, leaving the major burghs in the Borders the furthest distance of any significantly sized settlements in Great Britain from railway stations. (Hawick for example was left 45 miles adrift from a station.) The railway was earmarked for closure in Lord Beeching's famous (infamous?) report of 1963 but survived until January 1969 when the last trains crept their way along a line where demonstrators were out in large numbers protesting at the closure. At one station the level crossing gates had been forcibly closed across the track by local people, for example.

In hindsight the Waverley Route seems to have been mighty unlucky. The year earlier the Labour government's Minister of Transport Barbara Castle had shepherded through a Transport Act which released the railway network from the task of being run entirely as a commercial business and which recognised that railways also performed a social role. Other threatened railways were reprieved as a consequence of this changed thinking but somehow the Waverley Route closure went ahead, despite obvious concern from the then Secretary of State for Scotland and despite a growing community campaign locally to keep the railway open. Perhaps Hawick, Melrose and Galashiels were simply too far geographically from the centre of political power at Westminster.

So the story of the railway came to an end in 1969. Except that it turned out that this wasn't quite the end of the story. Passenger services returned to the northern section of the newly-renamed Borders Railway in September 2015, with new stations spread out along the line south from Edinburgh as far as Stow, Galashiels and the terminus at Tweedbank, thirty miles away. The story of the reopening of the Borders Railway has been widely told, but it should perhaps be remembered that this was by no means a straightforward affair. Numerous critics at the time condemned the whole idea. Indeed its reopening can be pinned fairly and squarely on direct community pressure: "The push for reinstatement came not from the rail industry or government but from local campaigners" is the assessment of railway consultant Peter Heubeck.

Patience is clearly needed in community campaigning. Years went by after 2000 when the new Scottish Parliament first held a debate on the proposal and a strategy group was established to prepare a business case. All sorts of issues arose and all sorts of difficulties were raised. The contract to build was only signed by the Scottish government in late 2012. Given that the construction work included among other things tunnelling under the Edinburgh by-pass, creating a new alignment of the railway nearby to avoid roads and mining subsidence, and building or reconstructing 42 bridges its completion three years later seems pretty good going.

In the years since 2015 the railway has been a runaway success.

Passenger numbers, particularly from Stow, Galashiels and Tweedbank, have been far higher than originally forecast. People have started complaining because the trains have been overcrowded.

These problems of success are partly because compromises had to be made to make the Borders Railway happen at all. For example, most of the line was constructed as single-track and the proposed number of passing loops was cut back. Perhaps the most significant decision, however, was the one that saw the line terminating at Tweedbank rather than continuing the short extra distance to that Category A. station at Melrose. The towns of Newtown St Boswells and Hawick, further on down the old Waverley Route, were also left unserved.

For Marion Short, this means that the job is only half completed. Marion is the current Chair of the Campaign for Borders Rail which, flushed with its earlier success, has been mobilising to get the railway restored *all* the way to Carlisle. Marion and Peter Heubeck (who is now providing his professional railway experience to the campaign) told me why they feel that their case is a strong one.

Unlike the early battles, there now seems to be overwhelming consensus among Scottish politicians that a detailed feasibility study should be done as the first stage towards a possible future restoration. Indeed £10m funding for such a study has been promised from government sources. Peter urges caution until the study is commissioned and completed but it's noticeable that he carefully refers to the Tweedbank reopening as 'Phase I'. Who wants to leave a project like this hanging, with only the first part undertaken?

Nevertheless, restoring a railway once it is closed (and particularly once the track-bed has been sold off) is not cheap. The Tweedbank reopening cost about £353m, and costs have increased since then. One helpful factor is that restoring the line to Newtown St Boswells and Hawick is reckoned to be less challenging technically than 'Phase I', although the Melrose bypass occupies some of the old solum near the town centre (and Melrose station is currently occupied by rather a nice Italian restaurant). Beyond Hawick is a different story: there are miles of empty countryside and the remains of a railway which even in its glory days obliged trains to cope with stiff gradients. Passenger numbers here might be much more modest. However Marion talks of the potential for freight on this southern section: there's a real need to try to get the timber lorries from the great forestry plantations nearby off the roads and on to a more sustainable form of transport, she argues.

The case for Tweedbank to Carlisle in other words rests on a combination of potential freight needs in the south and passenger needs further north. It's certainly true that local people and the local economy in Hawick in particular could do with the benefits that would come from better communications. As with other Border towns Hawick saw some big firms in the woollen industry, long important economically, upping sticks and moving abroad in the second half of the twentieth century.

Indeed there's been widespread concern in the Borders at the decline of once prosperous market towns, and particular concern about depopulation. The official data show that the numbers of children and young people in the south of Scotland have been falling recently. Partly because of this demographic shift the area has been left with the highest proportion of the population in Scotland classified as dependent. Restoring rail links is seen as one way of helping to redress current challenges and of building stronger communities.

Marion and her colleagues in her organisation are lobbying and campaigning hard, and Marion says she is quite happy to make a nuisance of herself in official circles if that's what it takes. But, as first time round, a certain patience is also needed. Marion lives in Hawick and says that when she goes shopping she is frequently asked exactly when Hawick will get its station back. "I avoid the High Street now because I get stopped all the time," she jokes. "But at least it shows how interested people are."

What the Campaign for Borders Rail is working to bring about is what other voluntary groups in other parts of Britain are also working to try to achieve – the reintroduction of railway services which once were considered essential to the communities they served. As well as Borders Railway, in the years since the Beeching Report there have other success stories: the reopening of the Robin Hood line from Nottingham to Worksop, or the line from Coventry to Nuneaton, or passenger services to Okehampton, or once-closed lines in the Welsh valleys, or the railway in Fife to Leven, or (most currently) the Northumberland Line between Newcastle and Ashington, to give just a few examples. But many of these reopened passenger services were on lines previously maintained for freight. By contrast, the Borders Railway effectively had to be rebuilt from scratch. "It is easy to forget how radical and groundbreaking the 2015 reopening was," Peter Heubeck says.

There remain of course many Beeching-era gaps in the railway map of Britain which some people feel need to be filled again. Indeed the GB-wide Campaign for Better Transport has a long wish-list of places it wants to see reconnected to the network: Ripon, Caernarfon, St Andrews, Fawley, Wisbech, Tavistock, Keswick and many, many more. Their argument echoes what perhaps the 1968 Transport Act was trying to say: that railways play a social role and therefore need to be treated as part of the public infrastructure of our country. Reopening a railway can help strengthen a local economy, can expand labour markets and can help combat social isolation, they say.

Given the public financial situation, widespread success seems unlikely to come any time soon but nevertheless there's another argument now being raised by railway campaigners: that we need good, effective public transport if as a society we are to meet the 2050 net zero target we have signed up to. As the Campaign for Better Transport puts it in a recent report, "Transport accounts for more than a quarter of UK carbon emissions.... Investing to improve the extent and accessibility of the rail network for passengers and freight is therefore a policy imperative."

Our landscapes carry the marks of two seemingly contradictory aspects of human activity. Ever since we turned our backs on life as hunter-gatherers and decided to settle down and turn to farming, human settlements have been the dominant aspect of the way that the land is shaped: our houses, hamlets, villages, towns and cities are the most significant mark we have made on the lands we have inherited. But nevertheless there is also a fundamental human urge to travel, and because of this our communications networks criss-crossing the landscape are there to serve our economic and social needs.

Lord Beeching was convinced that roads and not railways were the future, but that future is now with us and it's turned out to be more complicated than perhaps he could have imagined. At the moment visitors to Melrose have to drive, take a bus or (like me) simply use their legs and enjoy the old paths and byways. But who knows, perhaps in the future visitors will once again be able to take a train. If so, Melrose station is still there, waiting for them to arrive.

Woodlands on the approach to the Pentland Hills

The Font Stane, the Pentland Hills

A modern footpath sign from the Scottish
Rights of Way Society (ScotWays)

Traquair House (above). Below: The approach to Newark Tower

Tam Lin's well (right). The Eildon Hills from west of Melrose (below)

On the Borders Abbeys Way near Melrose (above and below)

Melrose Abbey

St Cuthbert's Way waymarker (above). Below, the River Tweed near St Boswells

Maxton kirk, with the bench from Maxton's closed railway station
Below, Dere Street, once the all-important road north

The 'grave' of 'Lilliard' (above left); on the Border (above right).
Below, the countryside crossed by Dere Street

CHAPTER 10

EILDON HILLS

The dark side of history

You leave the town of Melrose under the railway bridge just beyond the station, find a small gap between a cluster of houses and take the footpath. There's a signpost to help you: St Cuthbert's Way, it says. The Borders Abbeys Way takes itself out of Melrose by a different route so it's a question now of starting on a new long-distance trail.

For a very short time at the back of the houses St Cuthbert's Way takes you down some steps. Don't be fooled. Almost immediately St Cuthbert's Way changes its mind. The direction is up. Steps and more steps. Up and up. And eventually, with Melrose left hundreds of feet below, you're on one of the most evocative landscape features of the Scottish Borders. You're on the Eildon Hills.

The distinctive shapes of the Eildon Hills have been fascinating humans for a very long time indeed, for the simple reason that they are made up of three separate hill-pinnacles. The highest of the three is Eildon Mid Hill at 422m. Eildon Hill North, a little to its north-east (and the closest to Melrose), is just slightly lower while away to the south is the third summit, Eildon Wester Hill. They are like massive molehills pushed up out of the ground by a race of giant moles, except that the summits were actually pushed up through Old Red Sandstone rock as a result of volcanic activity around 350 million years ago.

The three summits are a landmark which can be seen for miles around, particularly if you're travelling north from the Cheviots. They certainly attracted the attention of the Romans, because the Romans named their military base and settlement just beyond the hills after them. The Roman settlement carried the name Trimontium: Three Hills.

But long before the Romans came, the Eildons had attracted others. A hill fort was constructed on Eildon Hill North some time in late Bronze Age times (so, give or take, let's say about three thousand years ago) and was later expanded to such an extent that it occupied effectively the whole hill. It's about a mile in total if you want to make your way round the circumference of the outer rampart. Inside, the hill fort (oppidum is what we should call it, using the technical term) enclosed a really significant amount of land, over 15 hectares in total. Excavations have found evidence of the locations of around three hundred huts which would have been timber-framed and would have been erected on scooped-out patches of level ground. Perhaps 2,000 people lived up here when the oppidum was fully occupied. The assumption from archaeologists is that this was the most important centre of a Celtic tribe who lived in the upper Tweed basin and who were called the Selgovae. Creating and maintaining such a significant location suggests a highly organised society.

It's not clear when the people moved away from their oppidum on the hill top (the website from Historic Environment Scotland talks of only 'very limited excavations' on the hill so far), but when the Romans arrived here they made good use of the summit of Eildon Hill North themselves as a location for a signal station. All successful armies require effective communications and this was one of a string of similar stations spread out south towards the Cheviots, there to warn of any latent threats. Given that the Romans were at almost the furthest northern edge of their empire at this point, constant watchfulness must have been the necessary corollary.

I have delayed mentioning the Romans at Trimontium, although logically they should have appeared in the last chapter on Melrose. Long before the Cistercians and long before St Cuthbert, the Romans had a major settlement close to present-day Melrose. It's a short stroll from the town to find the fields where Trimontium was located, just below Eildon Hill North and close to the banks of the Tweed. It's an even shorter stroll to find the town-centre museum which tells the story of the Roman occupation of this part of Britain. The museum, run by an independent charitable trust and recently given an impressive make-over with lottery grant funding, also bears the name Trimontium. I enjoyed my visit.

The Romans occupied Trimontium and southern Scotland for two periods during their time in Britain, once before Hadrian's Wall was built and once afterwards. The first time was following the military advance northwards by the general Agricola starting in 79 CE when, aided by the construction of a series of forts and a military road network, Roman control was established right up to the Highland line. Trimontium was built at this time and remained an important base for around the next quarter of a century. Around 105 CE, however, it would appear that Trimontium was attacked and destroyed. The Romans withdrew southwards and Hadrian's Wall (built in the years immediately after 122 CE) marked the new frontier.

Some years later the Romans tried again, moving north from Hadrian's Wall and once more re-occupying lowland Scotland, including Trimontium. This second life for the settlement began from around 138 CE as part of the military advance which saw the Antonine Wall built between the Firth of Clyde and the Firth of Forth. The Antonine Wall had a very short life, functioning for only about two decades, but Trimontium continued in use until perhaps 180 CE, becoming something of an outpost. The Romans abandoned all their forts north of the Cheviots very early in the next century.

Trimontium has proved very rich in archaeological finds, the first Roman material coming to light during the construction of the Edinburgh-Hawick railway which cut its way across the site. Some finds, including the striking remains of a Roman cavalry helmet, are now in the National Museum of Scotland while others are on display at the Trimontium Museum itself. Helpfully the museum has also digitised the report of the first significant dig at Trimontium, undertaken by James Curle between 1905 and 1910, so that the many illustrations of Roman finds which Curle included in his text can now be studied online.

St Cuthbert's Way makes its way sedately through the little pass between Eildon Hills North and Mid but of course I wanted to get to the top of at least one of the summits. I'd stayed in Melrose the night before and it was still early morning. Hardly anyone was about. I put my rucksack down beside a patch of heather and, released briefly from its weight, I clambered through the earthworks of the oppidum. No sign of three hundred huts any more and no sign of a Roman signal station, but nevertheless a magnificent view. Eildon is special.

And some might want to go further and say that Eildon is magical. There's an early Walter Scott poem, for example, about how the Eildon Hills were sundered in three by the magical powers of the mediaeval

Scottish scholar Michael Scot, who gained something of a reputation as a wizard. Eildon also gets a significant mention in another of the traditional ballads which, like Tam Lin, Walter Scott contributed to his *Minstrelsy* collection. This is the ballad known as Thomas the Rhymer, or Thomas Rhymer, or True Thomas. I need to forewarn you that we are again back in the territory of the fairies. Indeed, we are back with the Queen of Elfland herself who approaches Thomas one day when he is resting on a hillside near Eildon. Here is how one of the versions starts:

> *True Thomas lay on Huntlie bank,*
> *A ferlie he spied wi' his ee,*
> *And there he saw a lady bright,*
> *Come riding down by the Eildon Tree.*

Thomas initially mistakes the lady for the Virgin Mary, but the Queen of Elfland soon puts him right. It turns out she has sought out Thomas mainly with one thing in mind: sex. "If ye dare to kiss my lips, Sure of your bodie I will be," she says to him.

Thomas accepts the challenge:

> *Syne he has kissed her rosy lips,*
> *All underneath the Eildon Tree.*

The consequence, predictably enough, is that Thomas is taken off to Elfland:

> *"Now, ye maun go wi' me," she said;*
> *"True Thomas, ye maun go wi' me:*
> *And ye maun serve me seven years,*
> *Thro' weal or woe as may chance to be."*

Different versions of the ballad are ambiguous regarding Thomas's later fate, although it does seem that he may have been allowed to return to humankind after his seven year stretch. The ballad is commemorated by the Eildon Stone, a large block put up in the twentieth century by the Melrose Literary Society, which claims to mark the site of the tree where Thomas met the Queen of Elfland. It's a place visitors sometimes want to see, and it can be found north of Eildon village and north-east of Eildon Hill North.

Unusually for ballads in Francis James Child's collection, Thomas the Rhymer carries the nickname of someone who we know was alive during the thirteenth century, his proper name being Thomas de

Ercildoune. Thomas had a reputation during and after his lifetime for prophecy (he is said to have predicted the death of King Alexander III in 1286). Scott offered the proposition that Thomas's powers came from his encounter with fairydom: "Whatever doubts... the learned might have as to the source of the Rhymer's prophetic skill, the vulgar had no hesitation to ascribe the whole to the intercourse between the bard and the queen of Faëry," he wrote in *Minstrelsy*.

Stories like that of Thomas and the fairy kingdom were a rich vein of romantic material which was mined not only by Walter Scott but also by his near contemporary, the novelist and essayist James Hogg. Hogg and Scott were friends, although Hogg's background was much more humble than Scott's. Hogg was born near Ettrick in 1770 and worked as a young man as a shepherd and farm worker. He had to labour to make his mark in Scottish literary society and had to accept the somewhat condescending name bestowed on him of 'the Ettrick Shepherd'. His best known work today is the novel *The Private Memoirs and Confessions of a Justified Sinner* which was published in 1824. However he was also the author of a short story called *The Hunt of Eildon*, probably written earlier and very much in the 'gothic' tradition which was extremely popular around the turn of the nineteenth century.

Hogg threw everything he could into this particular pot. There are the two beautiful sisters Ellen and Clara, turned by fairy magic into Mooly and Scratch, two white hounds who hunt for deer with the king of Scotland on Eildon. There is the attempted assassination of the king through a draught of poisoned wine, the king being saved only by Mooly the hound dashing the cup from his lips. We have the comic character of Croudy the rustic, who (in an echo of Bottom in *A Midsummer Night's Dream*) finds himself turned into an animal, in this case a wild boar. There is a mysterious old man who visits the king who is never identified but who would seem to be the Devil in disguise. There is love interest, too, between the main character Gale (a local shepherd) and kindly Pery, although Pery finds herself wrongly accused by Croudy of being the person who bewitched him and as a consequence faces execution as a witch. Further magic is necessary in order to release her, and she and Gale eventually find happiness together by being turned into moorland birds who fly away. It is all, as you will by now fully appreciate, an elaborate confection of entertaining gothic stuffery and nonsense.

There is however one aspect of *The Hunt of Eildon* which strikes a discordant note with the modern reader, and this is Hogg's report of the fate of women accused of being witches. Pery herself manages to escape the sentence of death which has been pronounced upon her, but others are not so fortunate. Hogg intended irony, I think, but even so towards the end of the story he tells us that "the king returned towards Edinburgh on the 14th of September, and on his way had twelve witches condemned and burnt at the Cross of Leader, after which act of duty his conscience became a good deal lightened, and his heart cheered in the ways of goodness..."

Scotland suffered several waves of witch-hunting in the period from 1563, when witchcraft became an offence carrying the death penalty, until 1736 when the law was finally changed and witchcraft effectively disappeared as both a crime and a legal concept. What happened in Scotland was part of a much wider obsession with witch-hunting which seized most of Europe during these centuries and which also crossed to the New World (we are familiar with the Salem, Massachusetts, witch-hunt of 1692 through Arthur Miller's powerful play *The Crucible*, of course). This was the time, in the words of the historian Hugh Trevor-Roper, of the 'witch-craze'. It was also a time when very many unfortunate women, and some men too, were found guilty of being witches and were put to death.

England experienced witch-hunts as well, but perhaps in Scotland witch-hunting was carried out with rather more ardour (there were waves of persecution, particularly in the years 1590-1591, in 1597, in 1629-1630, in 1649 and in 1661-1662). Certainly there has been much more awareness in Scotland than in England of this troubling part of our history. In England (and I admit that I'm thinking particularly of Pendle in Lancashire here) it's still too easy to find stories of witch-trials from this time being dressed up as entertaining tales for tourists.

Excellent academic work has been undertaken by the School of History, Classics and Archaeology at the University of Edinburgh who have sifted all the evidence that can be found in order to arrive at as accurate an account as possible of what actually took place. The University's researchers have identified the names of 3,212 people out of an overall total of 3,837 people who were accused of witchcraft in Scotland. This information has been converted into a database which has also been made available as an online map (witches.is.ed.ac.uk). I traced on this map the route that I'd already walked, picking out some of the names of those unfortunates who had found themselves labelled as witches. Let's allow at least some of their names to be recorded here: Bessie Ur and Issobel Haddock from West Linton, Anna Hay at Romannobridge, Helen Thomesone at Peebles, Margaret Johnestoun at Traquair, Marion and James Henrison at Selkirk, Agnes Gaston and Isobel Wright at Melrose. And many many more.

As can be seen from the inclusion of the Selkirk man James Henrison in my list, men as well as women could be caught up in the witch-hunting in Scotland. Nevertheless the vast majority were women: Edinburgh University's database is made up of 84% women and 15% men, with the gender unknown for the final 1%. And women could suffer particular humiliation during the judicial investigation process, particularly when it came to the so-called witch-prickers.

One of the beliefs held by those looking for witches was that they had made a formal pact with the Devil (often, for good measure, involving having sex with the Devil), who had left his mark on their body afterwards as a sort of equivalent to the Christian baptism ceremony. Finding this mark on someone who was accused of witchcraft was the evidence needed, or at least some of the evidence needed, to ensure a conviction. The mark took the form it was believed either of some sort of visible mole or spot on the body or alternatively of a spot which wasn't visible but which was insensible to pain.

Of course the mark might not be anywhere that was immediately obvious, so women who were alleged to be witches might have their hair shaved or be made to completely strip. To undertake this task became a kind of profession for itinerant witch-prickers who would be paid for their labours. About ten witch-prickers were known to have operated in Scotland. Later some of these men were unmasked as complete fraudsters. Some it seems may have used custom-made pins which had retractable ends and therefore which did not pierce the skin at all – so that of course the skin being pricked appeared not to feel pain.

Those people who were convicted of witchcraft might have been found with 'the Devil's mark', but often those accused would confess to the crime themselves. Torture, primarily in the form of excessive sleep deprivation, was widely used. Other 'witches' were accused on the basis of statements from neighbours (the witch-hunts provided an opportunity for some villagers to settle old scores), or were named in the confessions of other 'witches' during interrogations. One of the ironic things about the whole process was that an Act was needed in 1591 to allow women's testimony to be acceptable in judicial proceedings: prior to this the law effectively did not recognise women at all.

The history of the Scottish witch-hunts was first given serious academic attention by Christina Larner in her 1981 book *Enemies of God: the Witch-Hunt in Scotland*. Larner points out that this was the first time that women had been criminalised on a large scale. She also places the witch-hunts firmly within the context of the Reformation, a time she says when for the first time to any extent Christian beliefs reached those in lower social classes. Before the Reformation, she argues, Christianity had made little mark on the peasantry.

One implication of this Christianisation process was that folk beliefs in supernatural forces became caught up in witch-hunting. For those hunting 'witches', fairies became seen as demons, a kind of race of angel that answered to the Devil. Belief in fairies therefore became completely tied to the crime of witch-craft. Indeed, Lizanne Henderson and Edward Cowan in their book on fairy belief point out the irony that much of the primary evidence which they were able to access in writing their book came from the records of trials of alleged witches.

What happened to those accused? Witchcraft was a capital offence, and some faced execution. Because they were supposed to have been taken over by the Devil their bodies required burning, although usually the burning took place only after the victim had been strangled to death first. Not everyone accused ended up executed, however. The University of Edinburgh researchers very tentatively suggest that perhaps two-thirds were killed with others being acquitted, exiled or having had the good sense to flee first. In the Scottish Borders area there were 352 known trials of 'witches' and 221 executions, according to the recent local account by historian Mary W. Craig, *Borders Witch Hunt*.

This sobering period of relatively recent history has, as I suggested above, been explored much more thoroughly and thoughtfully in Scotland than in England. There's also an active campaign in Scotland which was launched on International Women's Day in 2022 to belatedly try to make some sort of amends. The Witches of Scotland campaign is calling for the erection of a national memorial, an official apology for those accused and a pardon for those convicted. The campaign organisers point out that Massachusetts has already done something similar to remember the Salem 'witches' – so why not Scotland? "Now is the time to record and acknowledge our history, to learn from it, and to vow to continue the work to gain gender equality," they argue.

CHAPTER 11

DERE STREET

War and strife

I said my final farewell to the River Tweed a little to the north of St Boswells. I'd followed St Cuthbert's Way off the Eildon Hills through the village of Bowden (locals accused of witchcraft: Bessie Cumroy, Grissell Murray, Bessie Morison) and past the old Waverley Route railway line at the approach to St Boswells to find the riverbank a little further on. By this stage the Tweed might not have reached its full maturity but it was already a powerful and impressive stretch of water. I looked (of course) for salmon but none popped up out of the water.

I took a path from the riverbank into St Boswells itself (accused: Helene Gastoun). This is an attractive little town which among other facilities boasts an excellent bookshop and café where I was able to temporarily remove my backpack for the second time that morning and have the mid-morning coffee I had been deprived of two days earlier at Traquair House. And then I pressed on, taking paths and quiet lanes to the very small community of Maxton (accused: Thomas Richartsoun, Helene Scot). My direction, and for the time being that of St Cuthbert's Way as well, was now to be firmly south-eastwards.

The target was Dere Street, which I joined just south of Maxton. This is the old Roman road which was constructed as part of Agricola's initial push northwards in and after 79 CE and which ran from York through Corbridge to the Cheviots, and then down to Trimontium and onwards to meet the Firth of Forth near modern-day Edinburgh. It was in other words the Romans' A1. We don't know what they called their road but by mediaeval times it had become known as Dere Street, possibly named after the Anglo-Saxon kingdom of Deira which was once to be found in the lands north of the Humber, in what today is East Yorkshire and part of North Yorkshire.

Dere Street is an extraordinary path for walkers, a green passage running on mile after mile after mile through the Scottish countryside which is almost devoid of human presence. The few fellow walkers I met were mostly End-to-Enders, more than half way through their journey from Land's End to John O'Groats. If you're up for this challenge Dere Street is the recognised way to start the Scottish leg of your journey, as you come down off the Pennine Way.

Apart from the section which is followed by St Cuthbert's Way (which heads off soon towards Kirk Yetholm and ultimately Lindisfarne) Dere Street is not flagged by Ordnance Survey as an obvious route for walking, and there's not much in the way of signposting on the ground either. But this is a long-distance trail to match them all. It deserves to be very much better known.

Dere Street may be almost deserted today but that certainly wasn't the case historically. Although records are few and far between, the evidence is that in mediaeval times this was the primary communications artery between England and Scotland. We know that Edward I brought his army this way in 1298 on their way to fight the Scots under William Wallace at the Battle of Falkirk. The battle, in what is known as the First War of Scottish Independence, went the English way and Edward occupied Stirling afterwards before withdrawing back to Carlisle a short time later.

Warfare between England and Scotland continued regularly and Edward I's son Edward II also brought an army up Dere Street in 1314 on his way to the Battle of Bannockburn – a battle which, as everyone knows, saw the Scots under Robert the Bruce win a decisive victory.

A rather smaller skirmish, again between the Scots and the English, took place more than two centuries later, more or less on the line of Dere Street itself and close to an old stone known as Lilliot Cross or Lylliot Cross. The site of the Battle of Ancrum Moor is today marked by a board recounting the story of the battle. Behind the board, just off the Dere Street path, is a stone 'tomb', the resting place (allegedly) of a woman called Lilliard who was (allegedly) one of the warriors on the victorious Scottish side. A metal plaque by the grave carries the following tale:

> "A local lass from Maxton followed her lover to the battle of
> Ancrum Moor. Sword in hand she bravely fought the English, her
> epic deeds being immortalised in this verse:

Fair maiden Lilliard lies under this stane,
Little was her stature, but great was her fame,
On the English loons she laid mony thumps
And when her legs were off she fought upon her stumps."

Sir Walter Scott, it can be added, was one of those who made the most of the Lilliard story. It is certainly quite a story. It is also of course a myth (Lilliard's name almost certainly comes from the old name Lilliot Cross). Nevertheless Lilliard's would-be grave is the only obvious 'visitor attraction' to stop at during all the long miles that Dere Street cuts its way through the landscape.

There have been so many centuries of conflict and destruction hereabouts. Although the border between Scotland and England was fixed as far back as 1237 in the Treaty of York it did not end cross-border hostility. (To be absolutely correct, the Treaty of York drew the border along the Tweed and the Cheviots and confirmed Northumberland as part of England but it did leave unresolved the border line through a very small area further west, the so-called 'debatable land'.) Perhaps the Borders battle which has become most symbolic of the terrible cost of all this quarrelling took place in September 1513 about three miles south of the border, close to the Northumberland village of Branxton.

The Battle of Flodden, or simply Flodden Field, was the largest battle numerically between Scottish and English forces: estimates suggest that the English army numbered about 26,000 while the Scottish army was significantly larger. However the Scots' advantage was lost to them when they found themselves struggling through an area of marshland, and victory at the day's end was with the English. The Scottish king James IV who had been leading his men into battle was killed along with very many thousands of others, on both sides but particularly on the Scottish side. Flodden Field casts a long shadow even today. The haunting pipe-tune the Flowers of the Forest which commemorated the Scottish defeat is still played today at funerals and services of remembrance – and many pipers choose not to play it for any other occasion.

We live in more law-abiding times. Nevertheless, even though the border simply separates two component parts of the United Kingdom (at the time of writing, of course – who knows about the future?), you could argue that the reality of the border continues to have a negative effect on the local economies of both sides of the divide. Borderlands, wherever they are in the world, tend to be places where economic life seeps away towards places closer to the centres of political power.

Long centuries before Flodden, long before Ancrum Moor, and many centuries too before the armies of Edward I and Edward II used Dere Street, another group of warriors may very well have also used the old Roman road on their way south. This is the moment to make good the promise I made in the first chapter of this book. I need to take you back to the 'Dark Ages' and to introduce you to Aneirin.

Aneirin is remembered as one of the great early mediaeval Welsh poets, the "prince of bards" as one early Welsh text put it, and his time on earth was some fourteen hundred years or more before my own. As something of a miracle, however, some of his work has survived. In particular his great poem *Y Gododdin* is safely preserved in Cardiff, the text written down in a manuscript by two scribes several centuries after his death.

Y Gododdin is a poem of its time, an epic poem written – or rather composed, because Aneirin created his poems orally – to commemorate the warriors who fought and died in a battle which took place probably around 570 CE. The poem takes its name from the name of the Celtic tribe who lived in Aneirin's day in what today is the Lothians area of Scotland, and Aneirin wrote in the language which, as I mentioned when I was in the Pentland Hills, was until the seventh century spoken across much of southern Scotland, the language which at that time was turning into what would become modern Welsh, Cornish and Breton as well as Cumbric, the now unrecoverable Celtic language of Cumbria. Most academics describe the language of *Y Gododdin* as 'Old Welsh' but as it was almost certainly originally composed in what is today Scotland the Celtic scholar Kenneth Jackson described it (perhaps a little cheekily) in his 1969 translation as 'Scotland's oldest poem'.

The Gododdin's story begins in Edinburgh, at 'Din Eidyn' – the Fort of Eidyn – or in other words at what would in due course become Edinburgh Castle. The warriors who were remembered, praised and mourned by Aneirin had been feasting there, drinking mead and wine and enjoying the hospitality of the Gododdin people. In exchange, when the time came they had to pay back the hospitality by going to war. They left the fort to travel, to do battle and (in most cases, according to Aneirin) to lose their lives at a battle at a place called Catraeth. *Gwyr a aeth Gatraeth*, the poet sings repeatedly: *Men went to Catraeth*.

According to Aneirin there were three hundred warriors who made the journey (or maybe it was 303 or 363, there are some discrepancies in the Cardiff manuscript). Of these, only one person survived to return from Catraeth – or possibly it was three. Perhaps Aneirin the poet himself had joined the party and was one of the survivors, or perhaps not – again, there are different ways of interpreting *Y Gododdin's* verses. As I've said, this was an orally composed work and the version we have was only written down several centuries later.

Where was Catraeth? Jackson was in no doubt that the battle they fought was at what is modern day Catterick. In this he was following the opinion of the earlier Welsh scholar Sir Ifor Williams, and over the years other academics have agreed with them both. Of course we can never know for sure and it has to be said that others who specialise in this corner of academia are not convinced. If you want to be on the safe side you can follow the lead of Welsh poet Gillian Clarke who has recently translated *Y Gododdin* into English and who writes that Catraeth is 'probably' Catterick.

And who were they fighting? Jackson convinced himself that the poem recounted how a pan-Celtic army was trying to stop the Anglo-Saxon encroachment of the eastern side of the country. But his reading of the Gododdin story has been fairly firmly rejected in the years since he was writing. The 'cowboys and Indians' scenario of Dark Ages Britain, with the Anglo-Saxons conquering the plucky but doomed Celts, isn't an accurate one we're told.

John T. Koch, one of today's most eminent *Y Gododdin* scholars, argues that this wasn't a conflict based on ethnicity. "I now believe that the more important division in the sixth century was not the Welsh West against the Anglo-Saxon East, but the surviving ancient division between an ethnically mixed extramural North (the precursor of Scotland) and an ethnically mixed intramural South (the old Roman province)," Koch writes, referring to the significance of Hadrian's Wall as a boundary. Indeed Koch has put forward the theory that perhaps the real enemy being faced at Catraeth was Urien, the powerful ruler at the time of the Celtic kingdom of Rheged (modern day Cumbria and parts of Dumfries and Galloway).

So if Catraeth is 'probably' Catterick how might the Gododdin army have travelled there? Jackson thought that the warriors would have wanted to steer well clear of anywhere near the Anglo-Saxon settlements on the Northumbrian coast and so would have made their way down the western, Celtic, side of the country (basically taking the

M74 and M6 route south, in modern parlance). But follow Koch's thesis and just the opposite would have been true: the Gododdin squad would definitely have wanted to avoid anywhere near Rheged/Cumbria. So I like to think that they would have chosen the most direct route south from England: they too would have been travellers down Dere Street.

The Gododdin warriors were going my way – or rather I was going to be walking where, many years earlier, they had probably also gone. As a small tribute to the memory of Cadfannan, Cynon, Owain, Madog and all the other members of the Gododdin band, I decided that I too would start my walk at Edinburgh Castle and complete it beside the Swale at Catterick. Why not? It was, as I have said, simply a whim but it felt like a harmless enough one. (I need to add of course that, unlike Aneirin's heroes, I did intend if at all possible to leave Catterick alive.)

I didn't imagine that the Gododdin warband would accompany me as ghostly companions and indeed I can report that none made themselves apparent. For all the long miles that I walked Dere Street I felt not a hint of a Dark Ages warrior horseman over my shoulder (or a Roman legionnaire either for that matter). But we live in an old country. Many, many generations of humans have lived on this land and adapted the landscape to meet their needs. We are the current generation, simply passing through.

CHAPTER 12

ON THE CHEVIOTS

National parks

I reached the border the next day, just about the right time to stop for lunch. I crossed from Scotland into England and immediately plonked myself down on a patch of grass to eat the sandwich and banana I'd brought with me. There was nobody else around. I was at the symbolic half-way point of my journey.

The evening before I'd stayed at Jedburgh, diverting off Dere Street just south of a little footbridge over the River Teviot to reach the last of the Border burghs on my route. I'd made my way to the campsite there beside the Jed Water (another river which has been causing problems in the recent past by flooding its banks, incidentally), put up the tent and then begun to look round the town. As in Melrose it is the exceptionally impressive ruins of Jedburgh Abbey which immediately attract attention. Jedburgh, like Melrose, was one of the powerful Borders monastic communities which King David I was responsible for establishing. At Jedburgh, by contrast with Melrose, the community was Augustinian rather than Cistercian.

A good night's sleep and then the next morning I was quickly back on Dere Street which was still firmly taking me south-eastwards. Gradually, as the Cheviots became closer, the countryside grew wilder. The arable fields which had been there near fair maiden Lilliard's (alleged) last resting place disappeared and were replaced by rough grazing land occupied by hardy sheep and occasional herds of beef cattle. Eventually, just at the foothills of the Cheviots, I reached the tiny settlement of Pennymuir and was reminded again of the military origins of the road I had been following. Pennymuir was the location chosen by the Romans for a series of temporary army encampments, the most extensive and impressive of their kind in Scotland. As at Melrose the Roman camp was built in the shadow of a prehistoric hill fort, in this case the one known as Woden Law, and indeed it has been suggested that the Romans may have made use of the Woden Law ramparts for practising their siege techniques (the hill-fort's occupants had presumably decided by this stage that they had better move on). The line of Dere Street crosses through the Pennymuir Roman complex, skirts Woden Law, and then carries on up the flanks of the Cheviots.

The border when you reach it is, let's be honest, an unassuming one. There was no 'welcome to England' sign to greet me when I arrived, and conversely no 'welcome to Scotland/fàilte gu Alba' sign for those End-to-Enders or others approaching from the south. Frankly, though, an unassuming border is in my opinion the best sort of border.

What was there, however, was a simple sign reminding walkers that they were crossing from one access jurisdiction to another. Rules for access to the countryside applying south of the border are less generous than those which operate in Scotland. Rather than the presumption of the right to roam freely over the countryside, subject of course to those sensible exceptions (page 9), access rights in England work the other way round: the default position is that land is excluded from access unless you're told otherwise. As I've mentioned, the Countryside and Rights of Way Act of 2000 was based on a detailed mapping exercise for England and Wales that demarcated open uncultivated 'access land' which, together with accessible woodland, distinguished it from other countryside where public access was permissible only if there was a right of way such as a footpath or bridleway available to be used. Despite hopeful talk of persuading politicians to extend the 'right to roam' that's still the legal position today.

Here on the open tops of the Cheviots I was clearly on access land. Not that I needed to roam at will at this point, because along the English side of the border runs Britain's first long-distance trail the Pennine Way, and it was going in just the direction I wanted. I finished my lunch and followed the path down to Chew Green, the equivalent of Pennymuir on the English side of the border. Chew Green is another memento left in the landscape by the Romans. It's a 'Scheduled Monument' on the National Heritage List, comprising the remains of a significantly-sized Roman fort, two smaller fortlets, evidence of other temporary Roman encampments – as well as, for good measure, the remains of the deserted mediaeval village of Kemylpethe and its chapel. 'Archaeological area' read the signs which are dotted somewhat randomly around the edges of the Chew Green site: no digging allowed, but exploring on foot welcomed.

However, no sooner was I in England than I was out of it again. Fàilte gu Alba: very shortly after leaving Chew Green the Pennine Way makes a brief foray back across the border into Scotland. It's only a passing fancy. Very soon afterwards the path turns definitively south and returns to England for good. Back to Northumberland.

And back too to a landscape which has been considered significant and important enough to be awarded national park status.

The Northumberland National Park was almost the last of the first ten national parks in England and Wales to be designated in the years after the Second World War. The Peak District was the first in 1951, with the Lake District, Dartmoor and Eryri/Snowdonia following shortly afterwards. And then one by one came the other five: the North York Moors, the Pembrokeshire Coast, Exmoor, the Yorkshire Dales and Bannau Brycheiniog/Brecon Beacons. Much more recently these ten have been joined by three more designations in England (The Broads, The South Downs, and the New Forest). There is a firm – if somewhat controversial – proposal to create a new national park in central and north-eastern Wales, and a further designation is also being considered for England.

National parks came in on the wave of hope and optimism after the experience of the Second World War in that key piece of legislation passed in 1949, the National Parks and Access to the Countryside Act. "The Act was arguably every bit as important as other landmark post-war legislation covering education and the welfare state," Andrew McCloy, the current Chair of the Campaign for National Parks (CNP), told me. "We talk about the National Health Service as a national treasure, don't we, but the national parks are in many ways a national treasure too," he added.

The organisation Andrew chairs, under its earlier name of the Standing Committee on National Parks, had much to do with putting the idea on the political agenda in the 1930s and it is still hard at work today pushing to ensure that the national parks meet the aims they were set up to realise. So what were (and are) these aims? In three words: landscape, nature, people. Or in slightly more words, to conserve the natural beauty of the national park areas and to enable the general public to visit them and enjoy the beauty for themselves.

We nearly had our national parks rather a lot earlier than the 1950s. James Bryce, whom I introduced earlier in relation to his role in early access efforts in Scotland, had by 1919 returned from his stint as UK Ambassador to the United States and, now as Lord Bryce, wrote to the Times to propose that urgent steps were needed to protect areas of the countryside from being despoiled by "grave injury upon natural beauties which we owe it to posterity to preserve". Perhaps Bryce had been thinking as he wrote of the situation in the US, where the US National Parks Service had been established in 1916 and where the first of the country's national parks (Yellowstone) had been created as far back as 1872. Certainly the later British campaign for national parks was to be strongly influenced by the US model, in which the role played by the Scottish-American John Muir was a leading one. Canada too had national parks very early (the Banff National Park, set up in 1885, was soon joined by several others), as did New Zealand and South Africa.

The minority Labour government of 1929 nearly added Britain to this list. The Prime Minister Ramsay MacDonald, having been successfully lobbied by the Council for the Preservation of Rural England (CPRE), asked the experienced politician Christopher Addison to lead a 'National Park Committee'. The Addison Committee's very positive report in 1931 was well received but then almost immediately came the financial crisis, the fall of the Labour administration and subsequent savage cuts to public spending. It would be left to campaigners to keep the idea alive.

In fact, let's be blunt: it was thanks to sustained bottom-up campaigning by committed people that the national parks we can enjoy today came about. The Standing Committee on National Parks, established in 1934, was a partnership led by the CPRE which also brought in organisations such as the Ramblers' Association, the Youth Hostels Association, the RSPB, the National Trust and (an unlikely bedfellow today, but perhaps less unlikely in the pioneering days of motoring) the AA. The work of the campaigners during the later years of the 1930s included a short proselytising film for showing in cinemas which was produced in 1938 and can still be watched today on YouTube, and a mass-produced pamphlet published the same year, *The Case for National Parks in Great Britain*.

The pamphlet's author was the man who, more than anyone else, is credited today as the visionary who successfully got us our national parks. John Dower, in his late thirties in 1938, was an architect by profession who became central to the campaign. In 1939 for example he drafted a briefing note on how a national parks Bill could be framed. He joined the Royal Engineers when war broke out in 1939 but had to be invalided out and then, through one of those quirks of fate which are probably only possible in war circumstances, he found himself employed as a civil servant, advising his political masters on... how to establish national parks. The campaigner had wangled himself a backroom position exactly where he could make a difference.

John Dower's one-man report *National Parks in England and Wales* was published by the government in May 1945, the month when Victory in Europe Day was being celebrated. The timing perhaps could not have been better.

The 'Dower Report' is still worth reading today. Dower called for national parks to have two overriding objectives: the preservation of the beauty of the landscape, and ample access and facilities for members of the public to come and enjoy the landscape for themselves. Dower was adamant that the countryside should be there for all. The new National Parks should be "for people – and especially young people – of every class and kind and from every part of the country, indeed of the world. National Parks are not for any privileged or otherwise restricted section of the population, but for all who care to refresh their minds and spirits and to exercise their bodies in a peaceful setting of natural beauty," he wrote.

Dower's report was followed up two years later by the report which contained the deliberations of the so-called National Parks Commission, established by the incoming 1945 Labour administration. This 'Hobhouse Report' (named after the Commission's chairman Arthur Hobhouse) was somewhat more 'official' in tone than John Dower's solo effort two years earlier although Dower's ideas remained very influential (indeed Dower himself was a member of the Commission). The Hobhouse Report paved the way for the eventual 1949 National Parks and Access to the Countryside Act.

Dower and Hobhouse were given the brief to consider just England and Wales and the 1949 Act also focused on the situation south of the Border, but there was certainly the expectation after the War that Scotland would also very soon have its own national parks. In the years thereafter the issue regularly was discussed but nothing happened. It took the establishment of the Scottish Parliament to bring about the creation of Scotland's first two national parks, The Cairngorms, and Loch Lomond and The Trossachs. Galloway (along with parts of next-door Ayrshire) has recently been proposed by the Scottish government for the country's third national park.

Three quarters of a century on from the 1949 Act, how do we feel the national parks idea in England and Wales has worked out in practice? Undoubtedly lots of good things have happened. Many people have enjoyed the experience of visiting our most beloved areas of countryside. Committed National Parks staff have been on hand to welcome them and help them appreciate their visit.

But speak to those who today are strong supporters of the national park idea and you are likely to gather that there is a sense of some disappointment at what has happened. Some of the immediate post-war vision has evaporated. If he came back today Dower might not be entirely satisfied at how his idea for the national parks was working.

There is a sense that the democratic impulse behind his report, the idea that the parks should be there for 'every class and kind', hasn't been fully realised. The national parks (and indeed the countryside more generally) are not being visited by everyone in our society. Perhaps the strongest criticism of this issue came in the most recent government-sponsored report on the state of the national parks and our special landscapes, the 2019 'Glover Report' *Landscapes Review*. "If you grew up knowing how to read an Ordnance Survey map, or learnt the joys and sometimes miseries of hillwalking in the mist as part of the Duke of Edinburgh Award, or if you have retired to a village, the countryside can seem a very open and welcoming place, and it mostly is. But we don't think it is good, either for the countryside or for our society, that there are people cut off from the possibilities it offers", the report stated.

Those missing out, it went on, included young people especially adolescents, those in lower socio-economic groups and also people from black, Asian and minority ethnic groups. "It is as if access to the countryside involves joining a club. Those on the inside get the benefits. Those on the outside need ways in which to join," the report claimed. This is quite an indictment: the national parks presented as exclusive, mainly white, mainly middle-class clubs that you need to know the rules to gain admission to.

There's a challenge here for all of us to address, most particularly those of us who did learn early-doors how to read an OS map and who can be said to understand the 'rules' of the 'club'.

Other things anticipated by both Dower and Hobhouse never quite worked out as they anticipated either. Despite the strong arguments advanced back in the 1940s, a nationally-based and centrally funded 'National Parks Commission' was never given adequate powers to provide a clear strategic lead to our national parks' endeavour. Each park now has its own independent National Parks Authority, responsible among other things for local planning issues and made up of appointees and local councillors. Perhaps inevitably there is a tendency towards localism in the way that some of these Authorities work. Planning applications for house extensions, let's say, can take up a lot of the time which might be better spent in thinking strategically about the long-term management of the national park.

For a time in the later nineteenth and very early twentieth centuries land nationalisation had been a live political issue, with the Land Nationalisation Society as mentioned above (page 47) an active campaigning organisation. However the momentum behind that demand had very much dissipated by the post-1945 period and there was never an expectation from either Dower or Hobhouse that *all* land in Britain's national parks would be publicly owned. Nevertheless the Hobhouse Report suggested that its proposed National Parks Commission might in due course become the owner of 'substantial' areas of land. Indeed it argued that "some acquisition of land will be necessary" to meet many of the national park aims. This prediction also failed to materialise. I suspect campaigners for national parks from the 1930s and 1940s would be surprised today to see quite how much national park land is still firmly in the hands of private landowners.

They'd probably have been disappointed too that so much land in national parks remained for a very long time out of bounds to walkers. The Peak District park took an early lead in trying to secure access agreements with landowners (the Peak District was, after all, the area which had seen the most confrontation in the 1930s between ramblers and gamekeepers), but elsewhere other national parks seemed in no hurry to try to open up their countryside more widely to the public. It's revealing, for example, that before the 'right to roam' legislation came in early this century the Yorkshire Dales had only 4% of the national park's area open for access (it has since gone up to about 63%).

With no well-resourced central Commission to push the national parks' case at Westminster funding for the parks has also declined. The last fifteen years in particular have seen core budgets for the park authorities cut by around 40%, mirroring the swingeing cuts to local authority core budgets during this time. The Campaign for National Parks pleads for more resources to be found in the future, calling for a restoration of the level of funding enjoyed in 2010 and a long-term commitment for the next decade. At the moment, parks' core budgets are decided by central government on a yearly basis – as the CNP points out, this doesn't precisely help strategic planning.

So, starved of public funds, are there other ways that the national parks can finance their work? There is a debate in some national park circles about whether the answer could be to charge visitors some sort of entry charge for visiting a national park. It's controversial, of course. Andrew McCloy says that he is very wary of introducing charges. "If you do, inevitably you start discriminating, and you start barring places for people who don't have as much income as others," he says. But on the other hand he does understand the desire to find a mechanism so that people who are enjoying the national parks, and who may inadvertently be causing environmental damage to the most popular areas, are able to contribute something back. He adds that devising something similar to the visitor levy (tourist tax) being actively considered by some cities and by the Welsh and Scottish governments could be an acceptable way forward.

But then there's always the private sector. The British national parks have collectively started to sign a number of agreements with large corporates. All fifteen UK parks have agreed a deal with BMW, for example, which sees the motor giant put in electric charging points in national park destinations. (Mind you, there are those who argue that our national parks need fewer cars of any kind and more accessible public transport options.)

Potentially rather more large-scale is the partnership agreement signed in 2021 between the national parks and an international 'global impact firm' (their description of themselves) called Palladium. The partnership has been named Revere. According to the press release which first announced the deal, "Revere designs restoration projects with National Parks teams and land managers and raises private capital to fund the restoration. The projects generate revenue through the sale of ecosystem services, creating new income streams for farmers and landowners."

In case you are wondering what 'ecosystem services' might mean translated into English, I can explain that we are back again in the world of natural capital and carbon offsetting. Early Revere pilots include conversion of arable land into woodland in the South Downs and restoration of degraded peatlands in the Cairngorms.

It is too early to know to what extent national parks will be getting into bed with private capital in the years ahead and also too early to know whether, if they do, this will help the national parks realise their founding principles. The parks themselves will probably say that, if the flow of public financial support to them remains as modest as it has been recently, they will have little option but to explore new sources of finance.

There is certainly plenty of space at the border where Dere Street meets the Pennine Way, for example, for a nice big sign: *Welcome to Northumberland National Park, Sponsored by......* I wonder who might be persuaded to be the sponsor. Newcastle United Football Club? Nissan in Sunderland? The sign could be illuminated at night for night-time walkers. It is of course only a suggestion.

The idea of a national park in Northumberland was proposed in both the 1945 Dower and 1947 Hobhouse reports, although both envisaged their so-called 'Roman Wall' park occupying a much smaller area just around Hadrian's Wall. In the end, by the time the park was designated in 1956 it had had its boundaries extended northwards into the Cheviots. This has resulted in it having a somewhat less logical shape than most of its fellow national parks. It's also exceptionally rural: all the main market towns and villages in the area were left outside the boundaries, so that the largest settlement of any size is the little village of Elsdon with only about fifty houses.

The Northumberland National Park is also the least visited of the national parks, although there are some who would see this as a positive advantage: go to the Lake District, say, to find the fells full of fellow-visitors but come to Northumberland for the solitude. The Park proudly boasts that it was England's first International Dark Sky Park, an award made in 2013 by the International Dark Sky Association which is campaigning against light pollution. Visitors to the park on a clear night can drink in the splendour of the Milky Way or try to spot our own galaxy's nearest neighbour Andromeda, the light from which has taken a mere 2.5 million years to reach us.

The extension of its boundaries towards the Cheviots also had another long-term implication for the Northumberland National Park, and that is the fact that 23% of the land area is occupied by the Ministry of Defence's Otterburn firing ranges and army training area. The ranges were first acquired by the MoD just before the First World War and the land they occupy is extensive, 24,300 hectares in all, stretching northwards from the A68 almost up to the border itself. Slightly more than half the land is used for live firing exercises with the other half being 'dry' – that is, used just for army training.

Having military land in the national park clearly raises issues. John Dower himself described military occupation as one of a number of uses which would be damaging to potential national park landscapes (others were such things as quarrying and afforestation). The military should only be allowed in national parks, he argued, "on clear proof that it is required in the national interest and that no satisfactory alternative site not in a National Park area can be found".

The Northumberland National Park and the MoD say that it is their shared aim to encourage as much access to the MoD ranges as possible and the Otterburn public information leaflet says that "there is a presumption in favour of safe public access" to the defence estate lands. Nevertheless "this is balanced against the over-riding requirement for safe military training, the environment and local farming businesses". Military bylaws cover the firing areas of the estate and would-be walkers are instructed to keep out when firing exercises are happening, these times being denoted by red flags, road barriers and (at night) red lamps. The so-called 'dry' area (mostly the land north of the river Coquet) has been declared open access land under the CRoW 'right to roam' Act, although the leaflet advises that "the public may come across troops training in this area".

It's been more than half a century since the last time there was a substantive investigation into MoD landholdings to consider how the armed forces' needs could be reconciled with other land requirements, including the public desire for recreational access. Following the publication of the 'Nugent Report' (the Report of the Defence Lands Committee) in 1973 the MoD undertook to give greater attention to nature conservation on its lands and some public access was introduced in areas previously completely out-of-bounds. Nevertheless some recommendations of Nugent, including for example the release of the controversial firing ranges near Lulworth Cove on Dorset's Jurassic Coast, were later rejected by the government.

Little has changed since then. The MoD is one of the largest holders of land in the country today with a portfolio of just under 350,000 hectares of land (about 1.4% of the UK landmass) and with about three-quarters of this, around 250,000 hectares, in England. The Otterburn ranges make up just under ten per cent of the English land holding. The Roman army used this land. The Gododdin warriors may well have come this way, and certainly the armies of Edward I and Edward II did. And today this part of Northumberland is a landscape which is still dedicated to practising the arts of warfare.

The Pennine Way route, though it skirts the top end of the ranges, is always kept open although it has to be said that the 'danger' signs as you walk down from Chew Green (as well as the 'danger area' warnings on Ordnance Survey maps of this area) can feel rather less than welcoming. Overlook these, however, and the Cheviots here offer some fine moorland walking. The hilltops as you meet them carry evocative names: Ravens Knowe, Windy Crag, Houx Hill.

And then, eventually, the Pennine Way leaves the moorland behind and turns down through plantations to the Redesdale valley and the little settlement of Byrness, a remote community of social housing originally put up to provide homes for forestry workers. Byrness for many years boasted a YHA youth hostel. The YHA withdrew but the building remained, now turned into a welcoming independent hostel. The hostel (or more precisely the little lawn in the back garden where a small number of tents can be pitched) was to be my pleasant overnight stop.

CHAPTER 13

REDESDALE

Upland farming

The river Rede flows for over thirty miles through some of the more remote corners of Northumberland before eventually disgorging into the North Tyne at – logically enough – the village of Redesmouth a few miles south of the small market town of Bellingham. It rises as near as dammit to the Scottish/English border by Carter Bar and for much of its journey it chooses to be the close companion of the A68, the trunk road which I'd encountered at both Newtown St Boswells and Jedburgh and which would ultimately get motorists all the way from Edinburgh to the A1.

The Rede is a fine river, home to salmon and otter but also to another species of considerable interest to conservationists. This is the pearl mussel, a freshwater mussel which can indeed grow pearls and which can live for a hundred years – or longer still – if all goes well. For all to go well, however, the river that is providing the mussel with its accommodation must be clean and fast-flowing, there must be suitable fish such as salmon or trout swimming nearby (because very early in their life-cycle mussel larvae attach themselves to the gills of these fish) and human beings must be obeying the law and not trying to illicitly harvest the mussels. Pearl mussels have been protected in Britain since the 1990s but illegal harvesting nevertheless has taken place. River dredging has been a problem too, destroying the mussels' habitat. Regrettably freshwater pearl mussels are a declining species, not just in Britain but in other northern countries where they are found.

Recent years have seen efforts to reverse this trend in Britain. It's surprising what can be done sometimes. The Environment Agency runs a Salmon Centre at nearby Kielder where thousands of young salmon are raised in a hatchery to be released in due course into the Tyne and where in the past few years freshwater mussels have also been artificially reared. Given that tiny pearl mussel larvae are barely a third of a millimetre in size when they are ejected into river water by an adult mussel (and given also that the larvae only survive to grow if they are quickly inhaled by a host fish) the successful rearing of pearl mussels seems to me quite an achievement. Ultimately the mussels being bred at Kielder will help restock the Tyne and Rede.

I met the Rede for the first time as I came down to Byrness from the Cheviots and followed it the next morning for a couple of miles or so, past the settlement called Cottonshopeburnfoot to Blakehopeburnhaugh (place names are generously proportioned hereabouts). But all too soon the river and I parted company. The Pennine Way which I was continuing to follow took a firm turn southwards into the woods and the next few miles would see me tramping miserably on a dusty forestry road through endless conifer plantations. It was I would say the least attractive stretch by quite a long way of my entire journey. Things could have been better: in the very early years of planning the Pennine Way there was a proposal from local ramblers' groups to bypass much of this forest walking by routing the path along the Rede's riverbank for several more miles. Sadly their suggestion was not taken up. Perhaps suffering is a necessary part of the Pennine Way experience.

When eventually the forest plantations do end the Pennine Way continues its broadly southward trajectory over mile after mile of rough moorland. Bellingham (the pronunciation, as all Northumbrians know, is Bellingjum not Bellinghm) is the destination, but Bellingham is a long time coming. This is empty countryside. I don't think I met another human from breakfast to lunch.

More accurately, this countryside is empty of walkers. It is certainly not empty of sheep. Human activity, in the shape of upland farming, is all around. These moors and rough grazing lands are the workplaces for local farmers. And, of all the human interactions with the land that help to shape our landscapes, agriculture must surely be the agency that has the greatest effect.

It has always appeared curious to me that many people who enjoy getting out into the countryside from our cities and towns seem to have little interest in finding out how the land they are walking on is farmed. The sheep and cattle and the crops will no doubt be noticed, but *why* they are there, and why perhaps they weren't there last time you came this way, or may not be there next time you come, are questions that generally don't get asked.

That's partly because farmers traditionally haven't gone out of their way to explain their trade. Making a living successfully from the land can sometimes be so challenging and stressful that perhaps there is simply not the extra time or space in farmers' lives to try to communicate to the rest of us what is going on. It means that farming can seem something of a closed book, an esoteric activity that only the initiates understand and can undertake.

But surely there's an obligation on all of us to try to educate ourselves on the way that the countryside is farmed. So here's a suggestion. Just as you need to have passed a driving test to handle a car, in future you'll have to take a countryside test if you want to go out walking. It needn't be too onerous. Perhaps a practical element should be included, checking for example that you know to leave farm gates the way you found them and not to let dogs harry livestock. And then there would need to be a written test. I imagine the questions could be something like this: What began in 2018 with a report entitled *Health and Harmony*? What do the letters ELM stand for in a farming context? And the letters SFI? Can you explain the difference between Mid-Tier and Higher-Tier?

These are questions for what would be the English test. Questions for the Scottish and Welsh tests would have to be slightly different. But all three tests could include the really big question: How do you successfully earn your living as an upland farmer?

Well of course I'm not being serious with my suggestion. But on the other hand I do think we should all try to comprehend as much as possible what farmers do and where our food comes from. Sorting out our current environmental problems requires understanding and dialogue. So I would certainly agree with the environmental economist (and former MP) Alan Simpson whose blog I came across while working on this chapter. Our whole approach to the food we eat and the way it is produced has to be rethought, he argued: "We desperately need a new coalition between farmers, families and climate activists". Such a coalition would have to begin by guaranteeing farmers a secure living wage, he added.

Farming is in one sense a curious relic from a previous way of running our economy. For the last forty years or so our economy has operated on the basis that market mechanisms are the only tools we need in order to progress. Businesses and industries which can't be commercially viable shouldn't be propped up, or so it's claimed. This was the philosophy which saw British manufacturing hollowed out in the latter years of the last century and it very often seems to be the guiding principle today when it comes to much of our economy.

But not when it comes to agriculture. There is absolutely no way that upland farming in particular could conceivably carry on without financial support. It is, in terms of its ability to turn a profit, an absolute no-hope business proposition. So it has needed considerable public subsidy.

When we were in the European Union, this was something which didn't really need much discussion. As an EU member Britain was required to sign up to the Common Agricultural Policy, a keystone of the European project which at one stage took as much as 70 per cent of the EU's budget (it's now down to below 25 per cent, although in money terms that is still a substantial figure). There were very understandable reasons why CAP was created with such generous support for farming: all governments have to ensure that their people are fed, and memories were still fresh in Europe of wartime and post-war food shortages and rationing. The priority was to incentivise farmers to ensure that their land was as productive as possible. In a sense it worked: CAP historically not only delivered the food we needed, it delivered affordable food.

But with Britain's exit from the EU our participation in the EU's common policy came to an end, and there was an opportunity to step back and discuss why as a society we wanted to support farming and what the criteria should be for that support. Farming is a devolved issue, which means that the discussions and consultations which have taken place – and the measures to replace CAP which are gradually being put in place – have been different in England, Scotland and Wales, and in Northern Ireland, too. But certainly in the English context the key starting point was a report issued early in February 2018 at the time when Michael Gove was the relevant Secretary of State. This document (it is the *Health and Harmony* report I referenced earlier) talks of the opportunity to build a 'green Brexit' and to restructure government financial support towards a "more rational and sensitive agriculture policy which promotes environmental enhancement, supports profitable food production and contributes to a healthier society". In many respects it was a surprisingly radical approach to emerge from the then-Conservative government. The slogan was to be 'public money for the provision of public goods', with considerable emphasis on the importance of strong environmental protection including such things as improved air, water, and soil quality, increased biodiversity and measures to mitigate for climate change.

This approach was worked up into a new grant framework which was given the name Environmental Land Management – ELM for short – and since then the details have been slowly fleshed out. It hasn't necessarily been a straightforward process: as one farmer suggested to me, given the length of time the UK had been in the CAP, initially there simply weren't enough civil servants in place with the necessary skills for what their boss in Defra has described as the biggest reform in agriculture for seventy years.

The way things are shaping up currently in England is structured around an entry-level grant scheme called the Sustainable Farming Incentive (SFI) which the government hopes the vast majority of farmers will sign up for, combined with a so-called Countryside Stewardship Mid-Tier programme for those wanting to participate in more focused environmental outcomes for their farm. For a smaller number of farmers who want to embrace a more rigorous environmental land management approach to their farming there is the Higher-Tier Countryside Stewardship scheme, which requires more detailed longer-term planning for the whole of a farm and which also involves advice being taken from Natural England. The Mid-Tier and Higher-Tier stewardship schemes in many ways carry on from what were earlier Countryside Stewardship schemes under the previous grant regime.

Finally (because I sense that you want me to be as comprehensive as I can here) there's a third grant programme called Landscape Recovery, designed primarily for much larger land restoration initiatives typically involving either large landowners or groups of landowners working together.

Things are in flux and in five years' time everything could change all over again. But in the meantime maybe it's best to try to imagine a pizza restaurant which offers over two hundred separate options for you to choose from to put on your pizza (I appreciate that this would be somewhat unusual). Some of the options are available only if you opt for a specific pizza base and some of the options can't be combined (would you really want pepperoni with pineapple?). But within these constraints you can pick and mix to choose what's right for you. And provided you follow all the right procedures when you place your order the restaurant is prepared to actually pay you for each of the ingredients you choose (this is even more unusual, I know).

Well, that's my best attempt at a metaphor. In the world of SFI and Countryside Stewardship the options you can choose have titles such as WD12: *Creation of upland wood pasture*, and BE3: *Management of hedgerows*, and GS15: *Haymaking supplement*, and SW15: *Flood mitigation on arable reversion to grassland*. There are at present over 250 'actions' of this kind which a farmer can sign up to, although no farm will be eligible for them all and for some the options will be much more limited. In fact one of the complaints of hill farmers has been that there seem to be far more choices for arable farmers than for them.

I felt I needed to get a sense of how all these changes in agriculture, this 'agricultural transition' in government-speak, felt to those who were farming on the lands I was walking through. And so some time after my walk had finished I returned to Redesdale, this time driving rather than on my feet. My destination was the 247 hectare farm just a little way east of Bellingham, where I met Dave and Annabel Stanners. Could they help me to try to make sense of it all?

The Stanners suggested I rendezvous with them in the large barn just beyond their farmhouse. They were there with their wellington boots on, the visiting farm vet was there too, and so were about seventy pedigree Luing cows, a native breed of cattle which takes its name from the island of Luing off Argyll where they were first bred in the middle of the last century. Luing (you say 'Ling') were originally a cross between Highland cattle and the beef Shorthorn breed. Luings are hardy beasts, good for hill country.

Farm animals can get all kinds of ailments just as humans can and the Stanners choose to take extra measures to try to ensure the health of their livestock. The cattle were in the barn because it was the time for them to have their annual precautionary blood test for Johne's disease, a contagious wasting disease caused by a bacterium which also can affect sheep and other livestock. (Fortunately it can't spread to humans, although it does have some similarities with Crohn's disease.) You really don't want cattle in your herd testing positive for Johne's.

What happens on days like this in the barn is both mucky work and skilled work. Dave and Annabel expertly shooed the cows, and the bulls too, one by one into a holding pen at which point the vet whipped up each animal's tail to find the place to insert the syringe for the blood sample. (Later all the little phials, carefully barcoded with each animal's identification, would be heading off to a laboratory for analysis.) Each adult animal had to be tested which meant that any beast inclined to try to opt out of the experience had to be firmly persuaded not to do a runner. There was a lot of mooing accompanying the vet that afternoon.

Upland farms such as the one the Stanners look after are officially classified as 'severely disadvantaged areas', SDAs, and farming on SDAs basically means sheep and cattle. The Stanners' hectares include hill pasture and very rough grazing land, although there are also fields lower down where grass can be grown to be turned into silage for winter feeding. The Luing are quite obviously Dave Stanners' passion – indeed he was chair of the breed society for two years – and they are considered a breed that's particularly well suited to the type of ground that the Stanners have in abundance. But as well as Luing there are of course sheep on the farm, around 600 of them. The breeds of sheep change from place to place in Britain in the same way as the countryside changes and in this part of the North-East the Northumberland Blackface is a traditional breed, but farmers choose the breed of sheep that they feel is best for their particular farmland and the vast majority of sheep on the Stanners' farm are crossbreds, or 'mules' as they're commonly referred to. (Non-farmers should not be surprised if a farmer tells them they have several hundred mules on their farm – it's not what you might think.)

The lambs are born on the Stanners' farm from the first week in April and lambing time is the most demanding time of the year, requiring very long hours in often challenging conditions. Annabel Stanners told me that their most recent lambing was the hardest they had faced, with weeks of bitterly wet weather to contend with: farmers are perhaps more acutely aware than most of us of the way our climate is becoming more extreme. Lambing follows on a few weeks after calving which for the Stanners takes place in February (you can of course prearrange this by controlling the time when the cows are put to the bull or the ewes to the tup).

Dave and Annabel have run their farm since 2016 and, although the cycle of the year's farming activities follows a familiar pattern, each year is likely to be subtly different. Like all farmers they change and adapt what they do to reflect past experience. The female lambs are either sold for breeding or retained in the flock, while wether lambs (male lambs) are sold on to other farms on better lands for fattening up. The male calves (steers) are also mostly sold on to other farms for fattening while the female calves (heifers) are either sold for breeding or retained. There is a tricky calculation to make here. Is it better to keep the calves and lambs over their first winter on the farm or to sell them around November-time? Overwintered stock will normally sell for more when they come to market but on the other hand they will have required feeding over the winter months, and even with the farm's supply of silage this will mean buying in winter feed. Animal feed prices can fluctuate markedly and were particularly high after the Russian invasion of Ukraine, so it's not necessarily an easy calculation to make. The Stanners have in fact recently switched their approach and now tend to sell excess livestock in the Autumn.

The physical work of looking after your livestock, those regular round trips on the quad bikes to the higher grounds to check over the sheep, those days spent overseeing the calving and lambing, or for that matter those times in the barn with the farm vet sorting out the blood samples, are what hill farming is all about. Except that of course there is another aspect to the farming life that you also have to get right.

After the last of the Luing cattle had been tested and the vet had left the Stanners invited me to join them in their farmhouse and we sat round their dining table to discuss this element of their work. The government's 'agricultural transformation' necessarily affects them directly. Previously farmers and landowners benefitted from a direct subsidy payment known as the Basic Payment Scheme, the BPS. (In this respect it can be argued that farmers are the one section of the community who have already been trialling the much discussed social welfare idea of a Basic Universal Income for everyone). But in England BPS has gone, replaced for a few years by rapidly tapering 'delinked' relief. Instead farms need to look to SFI and Countryside Stewardship if they want to make up the shortfall.

Before the grant regime changed, BPS brought in a significant part of the Stanners' income, topped up with a smaller element of a grant from an earlier Stewardship scheme they had joined. Now that income has to be found in other ways. "The loss of BPS has really been felt by us," Dave says. "Hill farmers do feel a bit left out. We want to help the environment but we still have to be successful in our business and pay our bills."

A frustration, it rapidly becomes clear, has been the slowness with which the details of the SFI and Countryside Stewardship schemes have been emerging from Defra, particularly those 'actions' which upland farms can undertake. "Higher-Tier is the main option at the moment for us, and if we don't get into the Higher-Tier scheme we're really going to be struggling," Dave says. Their plans include undertaking catchment sensitive farming to protect the quality of the burns that run through their land, along with woodland creation including developing wildlife corridors. Dave mentions the possibility of using solar-powered GPS collars on the Luing, a recent development which when linked to an app enables the cattle to be restricted by virtual 'fences' and therefore kept away from areas such as watercourses or the nests of ground-nesting birds. "We do what we can on this farm, we need to be business-like but we're also environmental, we love going out on the farm and seeing the birds, the mammals, the owls, the bats, we love all that," says Annabel.

The Stanners have another string to their bow, having invested a few years back in an old British Railways mail wagon which has now been lavishly restored, placed on rails on the disused railway which crosses their land and turned into luxury holiday accommodation. This 'Wannies Retreat', helped by a glowing reference on a TV travel programme, is now a very welcome additional source of income even if servicing the needs of the visitors means more work.

So, all in all, Dave Stanners says that he is optimistic that he and Annabel will successfully be able to carry on farming. "You have to have a fair amount of optimism anyway in farming, there are a lot of downs so you have to celebrate the ups," he explains. But he adds that he is much less optimistic about the future of upland farming more generally.

Annabel concurs. "I think a lot of farms like ours will go out of business or lose tenancies," she says. She and Dave are very conscious that there are other ways that upland farm lands could be utilised. "I think the landlords will take over and do other things, like planting trees," she adds.

The point here is that for many upland farmers the land they look after is not their own – they are simply the tenants of a landowner. There is of course no easy way of knowing when you're walking the countryside or consulting your OS map whether you're on a tenanted farm or one where the farmer also owns their land, but if you wanted to guess it might help to know that about 45% of farms in England are tenanted, either wholly or at least in part. In terms of actual farmed *land*, about 70% is owned by the farmer and 30% is tenanted. This latter figure is higher in the North-East where there are significant large landowners, including the Duke of Northumberland and the MoD at Otterburn, and where 42% of the land which is farmed is under a tenancy agreement.

There are long-established Agricultural Holdings Act tenancies where farms can be passed down through the generations. However the law was changed in 1995 and now roughly half the tenanted farms in England are under a legal agreement known as a Farm Business Tenancy (FBT). Rather astonishingly, given that farming would seem to involve a pretty long-term commitment to the land, the average period of a new FBT is only just over three years (2021 data). Furthermore some tenant farmers are on rolling tenancies, up for renewal (or not) every single year. Indeed many of the concerns about the privately rented housing market which have been in the public spotlight in recent years, including so-called 'no-fault' evictions of tenants, apply in much the same way to farm tenancies – although outside of the world of farming they have tended to be very little discussed.

Obtaining a farm tenancy for farm tenants isn't necessarily straight-forward. Would-be tenants generally have to go through what is effectively a tendering process, preparing a business plan to show how they would manage the land and stating how much they are prepared to offer in rent. Often, nerve-rackingly, all those competing for a tenancy are invited to an open day at the farm, so you know exactly who else you are up against in the bidding. It's like a job interview where all the candidates are informally sized up at the same time.

The Stanners are fortunate to have a good relationship with their landlord who has agreed a fifteen year lease with them and who was happy to approve their plans to establish the Wannies Retreat railway carriage. Their current farm is in fact the first they have farmed (Dave having previously been employed as a stock manager on an estate) and before getting the tenancy in their native Northumberland they tried unsuccessfully for several years across the breadth of Britain. They recount how, for their current farm, they were interviewed and then invited back for what they thought was going to be a second shortlisting interview, only to be told that the tenancy was theirs if they wanted it: "I just burst into tears," says Annabel.

Farm Business Tenancies as operated in England received scrutiny in 2022 in a report (the 'Rock Review') commissioned by Defra and while this identified some examples of healthy landlord-tenant relationships it also highlighted abuses. It reported that "the landlord tenant relationship has become more transactional than relationship based", and it quoted one striking example where a landlord had sent their prospective FBT tenant a particularly starkly worded letter: "There will be no negotiation on the terms of the agreement. If you seek amendments, then the agreement will be withdrawn and the land offered elsewhere. If you wish to take advice on this then that is up to you but given the simple nature of the agreement I will require return and payment within seven working days." The review suggested that the 1995 Act had moved the pendulum far too far in favour of landlords' rights as opposed to tenants' rights: tenant protection had been eroded.

As yet no particularly significant changes have been implemented in England to address the proposals which the Rock Review suggested would improve the situation. By contrast, agricultural tenancies have been much more in the news in Scotland, where the Land Reform legislation presented to Parliament in 2024 proposes considerable changes to past practice. The proposals are designed to tackle some of the more problematic areas of the landlord/tenant relationship, including how rent reviews are conducted, how tenant improvements are valued when tenancies are not renewed, what compensation is paid to tenants when landlords take back land, and what rights tenants should enjoy if they want to diversify their farming activities. Perhaps predictably the measures are not uncontroversial. Scottish Land and Estates, representing landowner interests, have claimed that the proposals would strike a "grievous blow for generations" to the tenant farming sector. It is fair to say that lobbying from all sides is under way.

It's only about twenty pages since I crossed the border from Scotland into England and yet already Scotland seems left behind: I have focused almost exclusively in this chapter on farming in England. This can't be left unchallenged: something certainly needs to be said, if perhaps more briefly, about the state of upland farming the other side of the Cheviots too. As I have mentioned, agriculture is one of those areas of economic activity where powers have been devolved from Westminster to the Parliament in Scotland, the Senedd in Wales and the Assembly in Northern Ireland, and each jurisdiction is choosing its own path forward from the pre-Brexit days of the Common Agricultural Policy.

The Scottish government has clearly signalled that it also intends to link farm subsidies increasingly with environmental considerations. It is moving towards a new framework for agricultural support which it says will aim to reward "high quality food production, climate mitigation and adaptation, and nature restoration". Proposals for future subsidies (based on not two Tiers, as in England, but four) have been announced, an Agriculture Reform Implementation Oversight Board established and necessary legislation taken through the Scottish Parliament.

Farmers are being given clear indications of the direction of travel. However Scotland is choosing to move more slowly than England in introducing the new subsidy regime. It will be later in this decade before the transition is complete and in the meantime the Scottish government has been maintaining access to the old Basic Payment Scheme. Other add-on schemes that are relevant to hill farms, including the Less Favoured Area Support Scheme, are also being maintained in the short-term. Unlike England there is not quite the same immediate risk of farm incomes dropping as BPS disappears.

The debate over the way forward for agricultural subsidies is – or at least should be – influenced by the ever-present issue of climate change. Agriculture is a significant contributor to greenhouse gas emissions in Britain, currently running at about 11% of the country's total. The problem is not primarily carbon dioxide but two other damaging gases, nitrous oxide and methane. The use of nitrogen fertiliser, including leaching and run off of the fertiliser off the land, is the primary cause of the creation of nitrous oxide, while the finger points firmly at livestock (particularly cattle but also sheep) in relation to methane. The problem here is the way that the animals' digestive systems work. Cows digest grass by regurgitating the cud and as a result methane is produced. They can't help it, poor things, but about 95% of the methane produced by cattle comes from them belching.

There are other ways that agricultural activity contributes to greenhouse gas emissions, including the use of off-road tractors and machinery. The somewhat encouraging news here is that, overall, all these farm emissions have been falling a little over the past twenty-five years, partly because fewer cattle and sheep are being farmed than was the case in the days of European butter mountains and milk lakes. There are new agricultural feeds available for livestock which aim to reduce the methane burping. But having said that, methane emissions from agriculture have proved stubbornly unchanging in the years since 2009.

The National Farmers Union in England has pronounced that it would like to see farming becoming a carbon neutral activity by 2040, although they describe this as being an 'aspiration' rather than a firm pledge. The majority of farmers do seem to be getting the message (the Stanners for example have commissioned a voluntary carbon audit of their farming activities), but on the other hand the latest government survey reports that 24% of farmers thought it 'not very important' to consider greenhouse gas emissions when taking farming decisions and 9% thought it 'not at all important'. A further 5% or so said that their farms did not produce any greenhouse gas emissions, which conceivably could be true but much more probably just reflects wishful thinking.

What is currently being done in terms of reducing emissions tends to be around improving farm energy efficiency, recycling waste materials more effectively and applying nitrogen fertiliser in a more targeted way. There is less happening in terms of emission reduction when it comes to livestock.

So is the answer here to reduce stock sizes – to destock? There are already fewer sheep and cattle in our countryside than there were once upon a time and environmental agencies such as Natural England are keen to see further reductions, particularly when it comes to sheep on sensitive upland areas. Overgrazing is one of the issues which is addressed when Higher-Tier Countryside Stewardship agreements are being negotiated, and a farm accepted into Higher-Tier is likely to have to abide by agreed stocking levels.

The Stanners say that destocking is something they have been actively considering. But if you're trying to run your farm business to be commercially successful, it's not a straightforward matter. Fewer cattle or sheep means less money coming in from sales when you take your animals to market, so you are more reliant on grant income – and who's to say that, once the animals are gone, the grants won't disappear in future years? There's a particular issue for tenant farmers because, as they don't own the farm buildings or the land, most of their assets are held in the value of the livestock.

Nevertheless upland farming is, as we've seen, uncommercial so why not go the whole hog and simply stop farming these lands altogether? Get the sheep off the hills and use the land for something else – something that perhaps is less environmentally damaging?

Playing devil's advocate, I put this argument to the Stanners. It's an option, Dave admitted. It's true that upland sheep don't pay, he went on, but turning the land over to something like forestry wouldn't really make things better: commercial forestry is a monoculture, not precisely the way to get high quality environmental benefits. Dave paused: "And there'd be no community here".

Annabel picked up on this point. "It's all the things that go on in this area, the communities getting together, the children, the shows, so much stuff," she said. Without upland farming village life in their part of Northumberland would decay. Rural depopulation of the kind which other countries in Europe have been experiencing in recent decades could become a significant issue.

One of the benefits of the old Basic Payment Scheme, Dave Stanners says, was that it brought money to farmers which they then tended to spend locally. The money filtered down to other local businesses. If upland farming activity was to be cut back or even stopped altogether there would be wider ramifications: "Towns like Hexham will literally die," Dave claims.

A broader issue which is increasingly coming into discussions about the future of agricultural support is that of food security. Food, we've already seen, is considered to be one of the UK's Critical National Infrastructure elements. Every government needs to ensure that its citizens have the food they need and that the food is of the necessary quality for human consumption.

Food *security* is the catch-all term which broadens this out to look at, among other things, global food availability, the supply of food to the UK, supply chain resilience, affordability, and food safety and consumer confidence. It's a concept that is sometimes confused with food *self-sufficiency*, which certainly wasn't what the Corn Law reformers in the nineteenth century were trying to achieve when they opened the doors to cheap foreign grain at the expense of the home-grown variety. As I've mentioned (page 19), we currently import about 46% of the food we consume.

Nevertheless the world is a troubled place at the moment and climate change is bringing extreme weather to parts of the globe where some of our food is currently grown. It would seem a good precautionary principle to try to ensure that as much as possible of the food we eat is grown at home. It would also cut down on the greenhouse gas emissions caused from shipping foodstuffs great distances.

This is certainly the case which farmers' organisations have been making recently, arguing for food production to be more highly prioritised in the agricultural subsidy system. Their argument causes concern to some environmentalists who fear that the original imperative behind the post-Brexit 'agricultural transition' is in danger of being watered down.

Dave and Annabel Stanners feel that it needs to be a question of balance. Dave has recently become the chair of the NFU's North Uplands panel, a position which gives him the opportunity to try to bang the drum for the value of hill farming. ELM schemes should be designed so that producing food and environmental outcomes are joint priorities, he argues.

CHAPTER 14

HADRIAN'S WALL

Boundaries

About ten miles or so south of Bellingham I reached Hadrian's Wall. I'd left the Pennine Way after the first few miles and made my way by a series of footpaths and by-roads southwards. Eventually I met up with the old bridleway which at this point marks the boundary of the Northumberland National Park. It's not particularly well-walked and I followed it with some difficulty across Simonburn Common until I arrived at Carrawburgh – until I arrived at what was Brocolitia.

Brocolitia was what the Romans called the fort which they built here, one of sixteen of the large forts located strategically along the length of Hadrian's Wall. The wall itself, as we've seen, was put up in the years immediately after 122 CE at the time when the Romans were retrenching after their first extended foray northwards into modern-day Scotland. Brocolitia seems to have been constructed a little later than the wall itself, perhaps around 130 CE, and perhaps as an extra security measure to fill the gap between the Housesteads and Chesters forts, respectively a few miles further west and east.

Once upon a time Brocolitia was important. The fort occupied an area just a little under a hectare and a half in size, creating enough space inside for a garrison of five hundred soldiers. A high thick stone wall would have protected the site, and there seem to have been ditches outside the walls as further defensive precautions.

Numerous Roman inscriptions have been found at Brocolitia, including inscribed stones and tombstones, so that we know where many of the soldiers stationed here came from originally. At different times in its history there were troops at Brocolitia recruited from what today are regions in south-west France, in Belgium, in the Netherlands and in eastern Germany. Elsewhere on the Wall the garrisons of soldiers were from much further afield: we know that soldiers from Berber communities in northern Africa were at the fort at Aballava (Burgh by Sands) in Cumbria and indeed a plaque there today commemorates this "first recorded African community in Britain". The Roman army in Britain was ethnically mixed.

W. H. Auden's simple fourteen-line poem *Roman Wall Blues* very successfully conjures up the experience of the Roman squaddie on duty on Hadrian's Wall and although it's widely anthologised and you'll probably know it, nevertheless I'll offer here the opening four lines:

> *Over the heather the wet wind blows,*
> *I've lice in my tunic and a cold in my nose.*
>
> *The rain comes pattering out of the sky,*
> *I'm a Wall soldier, I don't know why.*

For Auden the landscapes of the northern Pennines were particularly special. In his wartime poem *New Year Letter,* written in 1940 when he was living in New York and pondering how humanity could extricate itself from the plight it found itself in, he called back into his verse "those peat-stained deserted burns/ That feed the Wear and Tyne and Tees" as his own personal symbol of hope:

> *An English area comes to mind,*
> *I see the nature of my kind*
> *As a locality I love,*
> *Those limestone moors that stretch from Brough*
> *To Hexham and the Roman wall,*
> *There is my symbol of us all…*

Brocolitia was first excavated by a local landowner in the 1870s, and much of the archaeological material found at the site is displayed a few miles along the Wall at the Chesters museum. The remains of the buildings inside the fort are now back under turf but the earthworks are visible and, almost two millennia after it was first put up, Brocolitia is still today an impressive sight.

Outside the fort in what was the civilian area, the *vicus,* is the *mithraeum,* an even more striking memento of the Romans' time in Britain. This is the small temple dedicated to the god Mithras, probably built some time around 200 CE. According to English Heritage which looks after the site it's probable that the temple with its small entranceway was deliberately built without windows: "This would have created the dark atmosphere resembling the cave in which, according to legend, Mithras killed a sacred bull and feasted with the sun god, Sol". I walked inside what remains today of the temple in what I hoped was a suitable reverential manner. I would eat my packed lunch somewhere else.

The 84 miles of the Hadrian's Wall Path which allows you to walk coast-to-coast between Bowness-on-Solway and Wallsend was given the status of an official National Trail in 2003 and since then has become a favourite for many walkers. For almost the first time since leaving Edinburgh I found myself sharing my path with many others. Unfortunately I had no more than about three miles of those 84 miles before I had to turn off to reach my overnight stop in Hexham, but they were three completely delightful miles. The grassy path runs gently through the landscape following the route of the Wall, the remains of which appear and disappear more or less randomly at intervals along the way.

Hadrian's Wall has been a World Heritage site since December 1987 when Unesco's World Heritage Committee held a meeting at the organisation's headquarters in Paris and agreed to formally inscribe it on its World Heritage List register. The committee clearly had a long agenda to work through, because another forty nominations for world heritage accreditation were accepted at the same meeting. Hadrian's Wall was in good company: among the other sites accepted were Uluru and its national park in Australia, Kilimanjaro National Park in Tanzania, the Acropolis in Athens, the ancient Mesoamerican city of Teotihuacan in Mexico, Venice and its lagoons, the Cathedral and Real Alcázar at Seville, and most of central Budapest. It was a particularly productive meeting for the UK which also saw the city of Bath, Blenheim Palace and the Palace of Westminster make it on to the list.

Out of interest I had a look back at the paperwork for accreditation which the UK government had submitted to Unesco in 1987: "Taken as a whole, with all its complex of structures, forts and earthworks of the Roman period, the Hadrian's Wall zone is one of the most significant complexes of archaeological remains of the period in the world," the submission maintained. The Unesco committee clearly agreed.

Since then Hadrian's Wall has been joined on Unesco's list both by the Antonine Wall in Scotland and by the equivalent fortifications at the eastern edge of the Roman empire in Germany, known as the

Upper German-Raetian Limes (*limes* here coming from the Latin for 'limit'). All three now share the same collective Unesco accreditation as the 'Frontiers of the Roman Empire'.

Of course Hadrian's Wall does deserve its special place among the most important records of human cultural endeavour and achievement. But it strikes me that, inadvertently, Hadrian's Wall's accreditation also records a rather less positive element of human behaviour, and that is the building of barriers and walls to divide us.

There has been a very long history of markers being erected in the landscape to separate *our* territory from that belonging to *them over there*. As well as Hadrian's Wall and the Antonine Wall Britain has the notable example of the eighth century Offa's Dyke separating the English and Welsh marches, but there are also many much smaller earthworks across the land which were put up to mark territorial disputes that have since been long forgotten.

Barriers encourage fear of the other and play on prejudice. And of course though the barriers the Romans erected at the furthest outposts of their empire have over time matured into their landscapes and become places now just of archaeological or tourist interest, the same impulse which was behind their construction is with us still today. We continue to have physical barriers to hinder or prevent us from travelling across the globe as freely as we might desire. (We also have non-physical barriers: such things as laws, and paperwork requirements, and lines on maps.)

The author Anita Sethi, who finishes the story of her walking journeys in the Pennine uplands of northern England at Hadrian's Wall, picks up on this aspect in her book *I Belong Here*. "It is impossible to walk by the remnants of Hadrian's Wall without feeling its resonance to our own era," she writes, choosing to comment particularly on Donald Trump's slogan of 'Build the wall' during his first Presidential campaign. Border fortifications today mean serious adverse effects on landscape and wildlife, she adds.

Walls of prefabricated high concrete panels, watchtowers, floodlights, minefields, but also biometric data, face recognition and other forms of digital surveillance – technology has come on since the Roman times and humans have developed new ways of trying to keep out the foreigner much more effectively that Auden's poor old Roman soldier on guard on Hadrian's Wall. The fear that barbarians are at the gates does not seem to have disappeared.

There are little boundaries as well as great ones all over our lands, of course. Look at any Ordnance Survey 1:25,000 map and you'll be able to see the lines of stone walls, hedges and fences marking out each field boundary, often going back to the period of Enclosure legislation. We may feel that the landscapes that we see when we go walking have been there for centuries but certainly in those parts of the country most affected by enclosure the field patterns and the lie of the land are comparatively new – dating back perhaps no more than two centuries. It was through enclosure that many commons and open field systems disappeared and individualised landholdings took their place: *my* fields, as opposed to *ours*.

Anita Sethi carried on along Hadrian's Wall to the Sycamore Gap, now sadly without its sycamore since the tree was wantonly cut down in September 2023. She feels the wind whipping through the sycamore's branches and she makes a series of wishes: "I wish for a world of no more wounding of places and people. I wish for a world in which we can all make a safe home and feel at home in ourselves... I wish for a world in which all are regarded as belonging equally and truly to this earth..."

The right response seems just a simple one: amen to that.

CHAPTER 15

BLANCHLAND

Grouse moors

It was a long day's walking south from Bellingham to Hexham and I was later than I expected in arriving. But there was a reward waiting for me. I'd planned it so that this would be my first night after West Linton when I would stay in a proper bed.

The tent did however emerge from its bag, to be spread out around the hotel bedroom. It may have been the middle of summer but nevertheless that morning at Bellingham I'd woken early to find a hoar frost on the ground. I'd had to put the tent away slightly damp. It needed an airing.

Hexham is a town with plenty of history. The focal point is the Abbey, which as in Melrose can trace its roots back to the seventh century. Here the founding father for what was a Benedictine community was St Wilfrid, the Bishop of York at the time. There would appear to have been little problem in finding the stone needed for the new Abbey church and buildings: the builders made use of what they could find close at hand basically by pilfering the ample Roman remains in the area. Let's call it recycling.

The Abbey as it is today is primarily from the twelfth and thirteenth centuries although the builders came back once again to undertake major rebuilding works in the nineteenth and the start of the twentieth centuries. The impressive East front to the church (which after the abolition of the monasteries was converted into the town's parish church) dates from this modern rebuilding period. The whole building has Grade I listed status.

The only problem with a bit of comfort in my Hexham hotel room came afterwards, the next morning after breakfast, when I had to shoulder the pack once again. For a fleeting moment I felt tempted to abort the remaining four days' trek and simply make my way home. I took a deep breath. That would have left the journey uncompleted. The river Swale at Catterick and not the Tyne at Hexham was the destination I had set myself.

From Hexham, after a short stretch of road walking, my route south took me into the valley of the worryingly named Devil's Water which at this point is flowing north to join the Tyne a few miles east of Hexham. Not so very long ago lead mining and smelting took place in the valley, so for many of the workers hereabouts life then could well have been pretty hellish. But the river probably gets its name from the Welsh for black (*du*): we are still in lands where once the language of the Gododdin warriors held sway.

I was following at this point, albeit in reverse, the route which Alfred Wainwright took on a walking holiday in 1938 from Settle through Middleton-in-Teesdale and Hexham to Hadrian's Wall, before he turned and headed back to Settle further west through Appleby and Dent. Wainwright wrote up his experiences shortly afterwards in *A Pennine Journey*, a manuscript which clearly languished for very many years unwanted in his bottom desk drawer (all of us who are authors have these, even if today with computer files the bottom drawers may be only metaphorical).

However *A Pennine Journey* did eventually have its moment, being picked up by a publisher in 1986 by which time Wainwright's beautifully crafted Lake District guides had deservedly found fame among all who love walking the Cumbrian fells. Indeed by the mid-1980s, on the strength of his Lake District books, Wainwright had featured in television series with author and broadcaster Eric Robson and had become something of a celebrity. Books with Wainwright on the title page were in demand and *A Pennine Journey* duly made it on to the Penguin paperback list.

Later in his life Wainwright had something of a curmudgeonly reputation, a loner who did his own thing in his own, very traditionally male, way. So it's interesting to meet up in his Pennine book with a much younger Wainwright: he was in his very early thirties in September 1938 at the time when he headed off on his walking holiday. He also presents a rather more attractive persona to the reader in *A Pennine Journey* than perhaps he did later in life, although there is some rather tedious business in the book about the girl of his dreams (and we only discover at the book's end that Alfred's wife and young son Peter are at home while Alfred is off walking). Nevertheless what gives the book its power is the way it communicates the palpable sense of anxiety in the countryside at the time, his own and that of almost everyone else that he meets. Wainwright's walk in the Autumn of 1938 coincided with the Nazi German annexation of the Sudetenland in Czechoslovakia and with the subsequent Munich crisis. The prospect of another European war was all too real.

I was making my way through the valley of Devil's Water towards the village which Wainwright says gave him the biggest surprise of his walk: "Blanchland, more than any other village I saw, deserves special mention," he wrote. "When you set foot in Blanchland, you step into the Middle Ages; it is its strange, mediaeval appearance you remember it by. You feel oddly out of place as you wander through the old stone arch and enter the square courtyard which is the heart of the village."

It's certainly true that Blanchland is a distinctive and unique place, one that is on many tourist itineraries. The Visit Northumberland website reaches for the hyperboles, describing it in turn as a fairytale village, a postcard-perfect village, a hidden gem and one of the prettiest villages in the north of England. We're also advised to ensure that we visit the village inn, the Lord Crewe Arms, which is 'oh-so-atmospheric'.

Blanchland is distinctive for two reasons: one is because in mediaeval times it was the location of Blanchland Abbey and the other is that the houses we see there today round the central courtyard were built as an estate village in the eighteenth century and therefore were designed as one, rather than in the higgledy-piggledy way that villages normally develop.

The history of the Abbey (yes, another Abbey, and so soon after Hexham) goes back to the twelfth century and although it was dissolved in 1539 its presence lingers on. The Abbey gateway remains in the centre of the village and the estate village was built in part using unwanted stone from the demolished Abbey buildings. The current village church is a partial rebuilding of what was once the very large Abbey church, and the Lord Crewe Arms was originally a guest house for the Abbey and can legitimately claim to be one of the oldest inns in the country. I concur that, yes, it is an atmospheric place.

However it is the fact that Blanchland has been for centuries a village owned by one estate that gives it its particular character. After the dissolution of the monasteries the land (as was so often the case) passed into private hands, and eventually in 1704 became the property of

Nathanial Crewe, Lord Crewe, a long-serving Bishop of Durham. Crewe on his death established a charity to take over both his Blanchland estate and land he had acquired on the Northumberland coast at Bamburgh. Lord Crewe's Charity is still going today and continues to own most of the land which originally came into its hands in Crewe's bequest.

It describes itself as a Christian charity (both the Bishops of Durham and Newcastle have the power to appoint some of the trustees) and its charitable objectives are primarily focused on offering financial support to Anglican clergy in the North-East, including helping them meet the costs of their children's schooling. Following Lord Crewe's original wishes the charity also has close links with Lincoln College, Oxford (Crewe's alma mater), offering financial support both to students there and on occasions to the college itself. In a typical year it has about £1m available for charitable ends.

About three-quarters of the charity's assets are held in the form of land and property, currently valued at around £42m. It was the charity trustees who in the years after Crewe's death in the eighteenth century developed Blanchland as a model estate village, and the charity continues to rent out around 45 houses in the village to tenants. It is also the landlord of the Lord Crewe Arms hotel, the village shop and post office, and the tea rooms. Blanchland is a village dominated by its landowner, but unusually the landowner that controls it is a charitable body rather than an individual.

Income comes in to Lord Crewe's Charity from the rent it charges on its properties but also from the agricultural tenancies it makes available to farmers. And there is another source of income: the two grouse moors it owns.

Grouse shooting is a controversial subject and one where many take sides. But since the use of upland moors for grouse shooting purposes is undoubtedly a significant factor in determining the way that landscapes look in both Scotland and northern England and since this is a book about landscapes I think now is an appropriate moment to pause to consider this particularly British activity.

Red grouse are wild birds which can be legally shot during the open season which begins on August 12th (what some call the Glorious Twelfth) and ends on December 10th. The vast majority of grouse which are bagged during this period are taken during days of driven shooting, an activity which as I mentioned earlier (page 21) developed in the middle of the nineteenth century. Instead of casually wandering on to a moor with a gun in your hand to see what game might make itself available to you, driven shooting is an altogether more organised sport. The shooters (the 'Guns') position themselves behind grouse butts while local people who have been employed for the day as beaters systematically progress across the moorland driving the grouse out of their cover and directly towards the waiting Guns and their guns. If the beaters have done their job a cloud of birds will pass overhead. Many shoots employ gun loaders to enable the Guns to waste as little time as possible before getting the next shots in.

A day's shoot will typically involve several drives of this kind, perhaps three or four in the morning before a hearty luncheon is served, and then a few more in the afternoon. The number of Guns in a party can vary, but eight is usual. What you will pay for your day on the hills varies too (depending primarily on how well-stocked the moor is with game) but – unless you are relatives or close friends of the landowner – the day is likely to set your party back several tens of thousands of pounds. Grouse shooting is therefore necessarily a somewhat exclusive activity, undertaken both by those with old money (the landed establishment) and those with new. If you are in the latter category and are coming up north, say, from your work in the City you will want to visit an outfitters beforehand to make sure you have the appropriate country clothing. Perhaps come with one or two £50 notes in your wallet too in case there are people who you meet such as the gamekeeper who you want to tip.

Just on the off chance that there are sceptics about this activity among us, I think it may be appropriate to start by trying to communicate a little of the atmosphere that a good day's shooting can entail. It so happens that Adrian Blackmore, the Director of Shooting for the Countryside Alliance, took part a few years ago in a shoot in Blanchland itself and afterwards blogged about his day for the Countryside Alliance's website. Here's part of what he wrote: "It's Monday 12th August, and the day that so many have been waiting for has finally come. The village square at Blanchland, on the Durham-Northumberland border, is alive with people of all ages as they wait for the beaters' wagons that will be taking them up on to the surrounding moors for the first day's grouse shooting of the season. The feeling of excitement is palpable, not just from them, but also from the Guns that are staying in the Lord Crewe Arms."

Blackmore's day consisted of six drives, with the last one particularly successful: "What a truly memorable end to the day this drive turned out to be, with masses of grouse coming through the line. Not surprisingly, as the final horn of the day was blown, there were smiles all round," he reported.

Of course the more red grouse that there are to be bagged the better the day's shooting. It is fair to say that there are not as many grouse these days as there were once upon a time. Several years ago when I was researching a walking guide to the Forest of Bowland in Lancashire I arranged to interview the estate manager for the Duke of Westminster's Abbeystead estate and at the end of our meeting he showed me what he called 'the bible' – the Game Book – with its record of all the grouse taken for each day's shooting back to the earliest days of the estate. In particular, he pointed out to me the entry for one memorable day in 1915 when the eight Guns brought down a total of 2929 birds in a single day.

Those days will never return, and indeed some recent years have seen grouse numbers so low that estates have had to cancel a whole season's shooting. But there are steps you can take if you own a grouse moor to ensure that the grouse numbers are as high as possible. The person charged with this task is the head gamekeeper.

What you want to do if you are a gamekeeper is to ensure that the grouse on your land are as healthy as possible. Unfortunately grouse health often isn't as good as it could be, with the bird falling prey particularly to an intestinal parasite called the strongyle worm. The remedy for this usually involves providing medicated grit to kill the worm eggs (hill walkers are used to coming across trays of white grit when they walk on grouse moors). The alternative method is to put medicine down the throats of the grouse although this does of course entail catching your birds first (it's usually done at night, by 'lamping' the birds with a bright light).

To maximise numbers in August ready for the Guns you also want to ensure that as few grouse and their chicks succumb in other ways in the meantime, and this is where a competent gamekeeper can really demonstrate their worth. Effectively a good moor for shooting purposes is one which is single-mindedly dedicated to the rearing of the maximum number of birds, and this involves making changes to the landscape in various ways.

It certainly means trying to remove as many potential grouse predators as possible. Once, for research for another book I was engaged in writing, a Yorkshire gamekeeper was prepared to demonstrate to me the tools of his trade. He showed me the wire snares which he set to catch foxes, the little traps carefully positioned on known stoat and weasel runs, and the Larsen trap cage into which he had put a decoy crow in order to lure in other crows, later to be killed and removed. These are all activities which are permissible under current English law and they can certainly help improve grouse populations.

What isn't permissible and hasn't been since an Act of Parliament in 1954 is the persecution of birds of prey for the same purpose. Raptors are protected by the law and it is a criminal offence to shoot or poison or try to trap them. Nevertheless gamekeepers are aware that raptors, while they predate on a wide range of small animals and birds, also take grouse and their chicks. Although successful prosecutions have been few and far between, the RSPB regularly reports on evidence of raptor persecution and says that since 2013 there have been over a thousand confirmed incidents – and they add that, because many cases take place in remote areas and aren't confirmed, the actual numbers are likely to be significantly higher. The majority of the RSPB's confirmed cases, around 70%, took place on land which was being managed for shooting. Not surprisingly the issue has taken centre stage in the arguments over the rights and wrongs of grouse shooting. Advocates accept that some gamekeepers have killed raptors but say that these are simply a 'few bad apples'. Opponents say that persecution of birds of prey is endemic to the industry.

One particular bird of prey has become the focus of this argument, and that is the beautiful hen harrier. I have regaled my friends almost to death about the time a female hen harrier took exception to my presence on a moor in the Forest of Bowland and divebombed me repeatedly (I wanted to point out to the bird that I was on a *recognised right of way* at the time but I'm not sure the message got through – communication was difficult) but outside this area of Lancashire hen harriers are simply not around in upland England in the numbers which they really should be. There were only about fifty breeding attempts by hen harriers in England in 2023, for example, certainly a lot better than the position a decade ago but still only a fraction of what you'd expect. Where are the missing birds? Well, conservationists firmly point the finger at those who are illegally persecuting them. They point out that (again using data for the single year of 2023) thirty-two satellite-tagged hen harriers were illegally killed or 'vanished'.

In his 2015 book *Inglorious* the environmentalist and campaigner Mark Avery looks in detail at the issues around grouse shooting. He recounts one case of an early morning on the RSPB reserve of Geltsdale in the North Pennines when an RSPB investigator watched as two men, one in a full-face balaclava, shot and killed a female hen harrier and stuffed the body down a nearby hole in the ground. The crime had been witnessed but no prosecution resulted – the men got away and the evidence was simply just not strong enough for a case to be brought.

So mammals or birds that potentially could predate on grouse are removed as much as possible from grouse moorland, in line with the law one hopes on reputable estates but illegally it seems elsewhere if those involved feel that they can get away with it.

However there is a further way to try to ensure that an estate has the maximum number of grouse at the start of August, and that is by making changes to the moorland vegetation. Young shoots of heather are tasty treats for grouse and their chicks while older, taller, heather bushes provide convenient cover for the birds. Gamekeepers try to provide a mosaic of heather plants of different ages by regularly removing older growths. This is traditionally done by controlled heather burning, or what is called muirburn in Scotland. A typical estate will have a regular rotation pattern for burning the different areas of moorland, the cycle lasting typically 8-12 years or perhaps a little longer. If you look at an aerial photograph of a maintained grouse moor you will very readily see the mosaic of shapes below created by this rotational burning.

Heather burning/muirburn is another controversial aspect of grouse moor management, particularly where the burning takes place on environmentally sensitive areas of peat blanket bog. Peat is an important store of carbon with the result that when burning takes place on peaty ground carbon is likely to be released back into the atmosphere. Furthermore, regularly burned heather moorlands tend to be dry moorlands, and dry moorlands cause other problems. They increase the risk of flooding after heavy rain (the water runs too quickly off the land) and they can also affect the quality of water being sourced from the moors for drinking purposes, so that the water has to go through extra treatment processes.

In England heather burning is subject to regulations introduced in 2007 which updated a previous regulatory regime and which are viewed by many as a fudge between shooting interests and environmental concerns (similar requirements were introduced a year later in Wales). Growing awareness of the climate change implications of permitting carbon to leach from peat led to the government in England tightening the rules in some respects in 2021. Heather- and vegetation-burning on deep peat (over 40cm in depth) is now not normally allowed where the land is considered sufficiently environmentally important that it merits the highest level of protection. This means being both a Site of Special Scientific Interest and also a Special Protection Area or a Special Area of Conservation. (I mentioned SSSIs and SACs briefly above, pages 61-62, and we'll tackle SPAs in a moment).

Heather burning can legally happen even in these protected places, however, although you would need to obtain a licence first. Environmentalists say that the new measures remain far too weak. Controlled burning is still allowed on perhaps as much as 40% of England's blanket bog peat habitats.

Critics of the English regime also look to what has been happening north of the Border where in 2024 the Scottish Parliament passed legislation to oblige all grouse moors to be formally licensed. Estates now also need to obtain a separate licence before undertaking muirburning and indeed burning on peat soils (regardless of the depth of the peat) is now only exceptionally allowed. The Act at the same time banned the use of snares for foxes and rabbits.

The legislation was seen at the time as at least partial vindication of the campaign against grouse shooting in Scotland which has been led in recent years by a coalition of campaigning groups called REVIVE. Under the Act those shooting estates which fail to meet the new conditions or which are linked to the persecution of raptors (Scotland has seen persecution not only of hen harriers but also, shockingly, of the country's emblematic raptor the golden eagle) should be at risk of having their licence to operate removed. Having said that, it would seem that skilled lawyers can sometimes find ways to sidestep legislation - the Act's apparent lack of teeth has already become an issue for conservationists.

Mark Avery argues that, ironically, these legislative problems in Scotland might end up helping those who feel as he does that licensing is only a poor substitute for the outright banning of driven grouse shooting. Since the publication of *Inglorious* Mark Avery has taken a lead in campaigning for this outcome, among other things by regularly using the Parliamentary Petition mechanism (this establishes that a parliamentary debate is required when 100,000 signatures are recorded for an online petition). Avery's first petition for a ban was launched in 2014. A similar petition, prepared five years later by the organisation

Wild Justice (in which Avery and broadcaster Chris Packham are two key participants), successfully crossed the 100,000 names threshold although as you might anticipate the then-Conservative government swatted down its demand very firmly: "Grouse shooting is a legitimate activity providing benefits for wildlife and habitat conservation and investment in remote areas," the government said.

Nothing daunted a further petition was being launched as this book was prepared for publication. Avery says that in any case he believes heather burning will have to be reduced as the dangers posed from carbon release from peat become more widely understood. That would hit the overall economic viability of maintaining land for grouse shoots: "It seems inconceivable to me that there will be much intensive grouse shooting going on in another ten years' time," he says.

So if you were to try to tot up the pros and cons of driven grouse shooting, how would your eventual balance sheet look? Advocates of the activity tend to stress the economic benefits which they say are brought to rural areas. Indeed Lord Crewe's Charity made this point in a submission to the government back at the time of Mark Avery's first petition, their submission arguing firmly for shooting to continue. The charity claimed that 'a very important part' of its income came from leasing out its grouse moors and that local businesses (including the Lord Crewe Arms) would risk becoming unviable if driven shooting were banned. This seems a rather over-egged endorsement of an activity which happens only on relatively few Autumn days, but nevertheless it's true that shooting does contribute to the local economies in country areas. How much it contributes, though, and whether it prevents other forms of rural economic activity and employment from developing is a much more debatable point.

Advocates of grouse shooting also argue that it is a traditional part of rural life. Those who criticise, they say, are urbanites who don't really understand the countryside and its ways of doing things. Of course, you could say in response that driven shooting is not *that* traditional, having come in only in the Victorian period. You could also argue, as Mark Avery does in *Inglorious*, that tradition by itself isn't necessarily all that effective as an argument: "If you sell your sport on the basis that it is natural and traditional, and people find out that it is anything but natural and causes ecological harm, then calling it 'traditional' just means that you have been doing the wrong thing for a long time," he writes in his book.

The ecological damage caused to the land is surely the real argument against the continuation of driven grouse shooting. This is why it has become a significant issue which groups like REVIVE and Wild Justice want to campaign around. While you might feel, given how many other problems our country faces, that this is a minor issue (only a tiny number of people get their pleasure on and after August 12th from positioning themselves behind a grouse butt) moorland habitats have to be effectively reduced to a monoculture to enable them to do so. Birds and animals are removed from the land and heather is managed as carefully as any farmer's crop.

Let's return to Blanchland. The Visit Northumberland website, after praising the delights of the village, goes on to stress the attractiveness of the countryside on its doorstep. Blanchland, it says, is surrounded by "magnificent fells and idyllic views". Indeed these fells, both to the north of the village in Northumberland and just south on the Durham side of the county boundary, have full environmental protection. They are part of a Site of Special Scientific Interest and they have received the two further accolades of being Special Protection Areas (SPAs) and Special Areas of Conservation (SACs). These, both in origin European Union environmental designations, respectively recognise the presence of important bird life and mark biodiversity and nature conservation significance. SSSIs which are also SACs and SPAs are, you might say, the crème de la crème of our habitats.

And sure enough, as I left Blanchland behind to take the hillside footpath towards Edmundbyers, the hills were alive with wildlife. There were curlews flying overhead. There were lapwings and oyster-catchers and many of the other moorland birds which you'd hope to see in countryside like this. Although I was on a shooting estate (the Muggleswick estate) the estate management had taken the trouble to put up signs advising walkers of the land's SSSI, SAC and SPA designations. Here was moorland countryside to enjoy to the maximum.

I have to report however that the moorland I crossed as I approached Blanchland from the north was the complete contrast. It was almost devoid of life, except for the occasional grouse. It was as though the land had suffered some form of terrible devastation. The track across the moor was well-constructed for 4x4s and I marched along it as quickly as I could: there was little pleasure to be taken by walking here.

Here was land, I told myself, which had received the attention of a gamekeeper who was very good at his job.

CHAPTER 16

EDMUNDBYERS

Water catchment

Heading to Edmundbyers involved me making a sharp turn eastwards from my trajectory south, but the youth hostel in the village has a camping field attached and I'd booked myself and my tent in there for the evening. Just like the hostel at Byrness further north, this is a former Youth Hostels Association building which the YHA has given up but which has been taken over and is now run independently. It provided me that evening with a welcome hand-pulled pint and a tasty pizza.

There was a second reason why I wanted to see Edmundbyers. My grandfather, who grew up on Tyneside, had enjoyed cycling out into the Northumberland and County Durham countryside as a young man, and Edmundbyers was one of the places I particularly remember him reminiscing about. It's certainly attractive countryside. Cycling there from Newcastle would have meant a round-trip ride of about fifty or sixty miles, which sounds like a pretty decent day out.

What my grandfather wouldn't have seen on his pushbike is today's most prominent landmark, because the Derwent Reservoir just to the north and east of the village was first planned only in the late 1950s and not completed and opened until 1967. The reservoir now provides water to the treatment works two miles downstream at Mosswood which in turn provides for the needs of Northumbrian Water's customers elsewhere in County Durham. It also acts as a visitor attraction. Sailing and water sports are allowed and there's a country park close to the southern shore with plenty for families to enjoy, even if the red squirrels in the nearby woods don't always oblige by coming out to be admired.

In many areas of upland Britain water reservoirs comprise another major human intrusion into the landscape but one which we tend now just to take for granted – perhaps too much for granted. Derwent Reservoir was in fact a very late arrival in the countryside. A century earlier by the middle of the nineteenth century some large city corporations were already well advanced in their work of trying to secure supplies of fresh water for their citizens. Liverpool Corporation for example looked north-east towards the West Pennine hills, receiving permission for its Rivington reservoir up near Bolton in 1847 and receiving the first water from there ten years on. Later Liverpool turned to mid-Wales and flooded the head of the Efyrnwy (Vyrnwy) valley, submerging the substantial village of Llanwddyn in the process. Glasgow chose to draw its water from Loch Katrine some thirty miles to the north, with Queen Victoria opening the completed works in 1859 (later in the century Glasgow was to commission further engineering work to extend Loch Katrine and to build a second reservoir near Milngavie). Manchester created a string of reservoirs in Longdendale in the Peak District between 1848 and 1884 before turning to the Lake District for additional reservoirs at Thirlmere and Haweswater. Bradford developed reservoirs in Nidderdale. Birmingham, like Liverpool, looked to mid-Wales, creating four reservoirs in the Elan valley at the end of the nineteenth century.

Not everyone at the time when all this civil engineering work was taking place was happy. The Thirlmere reservoir proposal at the time attracted opposition from a distinguished group of opponents including the housing reformer Octavia Hill (one of the founders of the National Trust), William Morris, John Ruskin and Matthew Arnold. The valley reservoirs in mid-Wales were (and have remained) very controversial in some circles, partly because English authorities used compulsory purchase powers to buy up houses and farmland with little if any attempt at local consultation. The Elan reservoirs involved demolishing a church, a school, three manor houses and several farmhouses. Very many years later, in 1982, during the period when English-owned holiday houses in Wales were being firebombed, someone planted a bomb at the Birmingham offices of the Severn Trent Authority as a somewhat belated protest.

There was also a period when ramblers weren't particularly happy at the attitude of the water authorities, or at least at the way that public access to the countryside around reservoirs was prohibited. Manchester

Corporation for example had 'Trespassers will be Prosecuted' signs dotted around its reservoirs in Longdendale, with wardens employed to turn back anyone tempted not to read the signs. Manchester later fought (and won) a legal battle with the Ramblers' Association to prevent the Pennine Way being initially routed on the lands north of the reservoirs. There were similar legal disputes in the 1950s between ramblers and Huddersfield Corporation over the land near its Digley Reservoir in the Peak District (Huddersfield lost), and with those wanting access to Boulsworth Hill in the South Pennines (the ramblers lost).

These battles took place in the days before modern filtration plants, which meant that large areas of countryside around reservoirs had to be acquired, cleared of their farms and kept empty for fear that the water draining off these gathering grounds could be contaminated. The rambler and activist Tom Stephenson, the man who more than anyone was responsible for the creation of the Pennine Way and who by the 1950s had become the Secretary of the Ramblers' Association, was not convinced. In his memoir *Forbidden Land*, posthumously published in 1989, he wrote: "Almost as rigorous as the sporting interests in their prohibition of walkers on the moors were some of the water authorities. To allow ramblers on their gathering grounds, they said, might lead to pollution of their reservoirs, and perhaps cause a typhoid epidemic. Some authorities, like Bolton, Bradford, Huddersfield, and Manchester, while banning ramblers, leased their moors for grouse shooting. The shooters, the keepers and the beaters were, presumably, pure and uncontaminated, or, as one rambler put it more crudely, they were a superior race devoid of bowels and bladders."

It was primarily municipal endeavour that enabled most of the houses in the majority of cities and towns in Britain to have piped drinking water by the time of the First World War. This highly significant investment in our country's long-term infrastructure was funded by equally long-term borrowing, with councils arranging loans via the Local Government Board and with repayments typically being spread over a hundred years or even longer. In the twenty-five years to 1897 £88m was raised in this way. Local authorities at that time appeared ready to look ahead and plan for the future requirements of their populations. Maybe today we have forgotten the lessons of that time: we seem reluctant to undertake the strategic planning and the adequate capital investment necessary to prepare for the times ahead.

The nineteenth century wasn't entirely a story of municipal water companies, however. In some parts of the country private-sector firms with capital usually provided by local shareholders undertook this work, using a model that in many respects resembled the way that new railway branch lines had been funded a little earlier in the nineteenth century. The major cities in England's North-East didn't have municipal water undertakings and the two important private water firms there, Newcastle and Gateshead, and Sunderland and South Shields, both continued to operate for much of the twentieth century. It was the Sunderland and South Shields company which was responsible for commissioning the Derwent Reservoir near Edmundbyers.

Reform to the water industry happened in 1973 when the Water Act brought together most of the many hundreds of separate municipal and private concerns in England and Wales into ten regional water authorities, creating a structure which later provided the basis for the privatised companies (Northumbrian, North-West, Yorkshire, Severn Trent, Welsh, Anglian, Southern, Wessex, South-West and – the largest of them all – Thames Water). The 1973 Act also saw control of water investment and finance move from local authorities to central government, a change which in hindsight didn't do many favours for the industry: the sums borrowed for investment fell significantly after the Act's implementation in 1974. A further Water Act was passed in 1983 by the then-Conservative government under Margaret Thatcher which among other things removed all residual local government involvement in the water authorities. Privatisation arrived in 1989, partly with the hope that private capital could make up for the lack of adequate public investment.

In this as in other areas Scottish history has been different. Scotland side-stepped privatisation and instead Scottish Water (the authority created in 2002 from a merger of the three previous water authorities in the country) is a public corporation, albeit one that is expected to behave as a commercial trading venture. Its performance is ultimately for the Scottish Parliament to judge. It can apply for public investment capital and as it has no private shareholders it also has no need to pay dividends. Wales is also different from England: Dŵr Cymru/Welsh Water is a company, but one which has been set up to be not-for-profit.

Those reservoirs dotted throughout the English, Welsh and Scottish countryside, many dating back to Victorian times, are the most visible manifestation in the landscape of the need to provide adequate sources of drinking water. However the task of getting water to towns and cities where the bulk of the population lived involved rather more than just reservoirs. The water had to be transferred to where it was needed and this meant that further substantial engineering work had to be undertaken. At the same time as navvies were busy building reservoir dams work was also going on to build the water conduits (the aqueducts) to take the water away.

The way that this process takes place today is based very much on the networks developed then, and the story is complicated. Sometimes natural river systems can be utilised: flows from a reservoir can be fed into an existing river and then extracted again further downstream. The rivers in our countryside rise and fall from day to day, but it may not only be the weather that determines their level – it may be water engineers who are deciding how much water to release or extract.

Very often, however, water is channelled to its destination underground through a series of large tunnels, often hundreds of feet below the ground. An upland area like the Yorkshire Dales, for example, has its own hidden network of tunnels which is almost as complex (and arguably just as important) as London's Underground, though most people who walk the countryside are oblivious to the feats of engineering beneath their boots.

What's particularly impressive is that the water often gets to its destination simply by using the force of gravity. Sometimes pumps may be necessary but Victorian water engineers tried where possible to avoid having to use them. The feed from Loch Katrine to Glasgow was entirely organised using gravity, for example. So too was the design of the Nidd Aqueduct which takes the water on an eighteen hour journey from Scar Head reservoir at the head of Nidderdale to the city of Bradford. (Where the water needs to be coaxed up the sides of valleys encountered on the way, the familiar syphon technique is used, although admittedly the syphons on the Nidd Aqueduct operate on a rather larger scale than most of us are familiar with.)

So there's plenty going on in the water industry, even though it may be forgotten and unloved by many of us. And what is particularly going on at the moment – quite apart from public anger about sewage in our river systems – is high-level concern that major new infrastructure is urgently needed. The National Infrastructure Commission is the public body which advises on the future capital investment which it considers necessary in England, and the NIC published a hard-hitting report *Preparing for a drier future* in 2018 which warned of major problems looming for our water supply unless significant remedial steps are taken very soon. "The Commission identified a range of pressures facing the water industry, including climate change, population growth, growing consumer expectations, ageing infrastructure and the need to protect the environment," wrote the NIC's Chair Sir John Armitt in his foreword to the report.

In particular, the NIC said that there was a one in four chance of a severe drought hitting the country some time in the years up to 2050. One necessary step to prevent systemic water shortages in the future is to try to persuade consumers to use less water, but urgent measures also need to be taken on the water supply side to increase capacity. There are various options, but one is certainly to build new reservoirs.

Very shortly after Derwent Reservoir was completed, now more than half a century ago, the giant reservoirs of Kielder Water in Northumberland and Rutland Water in the East Midlands also entered usage. But the time since then has seen little major reservoir construction. One of the many criticisms of a privatised water system in England is that private capital has not met the need for investment in the sector.

So now, somehow, it would seem that someone has to finance and build further reservoirs. "Reservoirs have significant capital costs and are generally most cost-effective when large volumes of water are needed. They can also bring environmental benefits (providing habitats for birds and aquatic species), as well as recreational benefits. However, they take up large land areas and can disrupt local communities," the NIC's 2018 report pointed out. And it added significantly, "Reservoirs must be planned well before they are needed, as it takes around ten years from the decision to build to being able to use the water supplied".

There has been talk of at least ten new reservoirs being required. One, the Havant Thicket Reservoir in Hampshire, is already underway while Anglian Water is developing proposals for two reservoirs in the Fenlands of Cambridgeshire and Lincolnshire. Thames Water is working on the so-called South East Strategic Reservoir Option (SESRO), for a reservoir in the Thames Valley near Didcot which would be able to extract water when required from the nearby Thames, and another proposal is for a new reservoir at Cheddar in Somerset. The particular risk of water shortages is in the South of England, particularly in London and the Home Counties area, rather than in the North of England although the North is seen as the potential source of additional water, to be transferred south overland perhaps via the canal system.

Will local people be prepared to accept proposals for new reservoirs? The problem perhaps is that the extraction of dividends from the water industry through the privatisation process has left many feeling anything but warm towards the companies involved. Finding a way forward for water that meets the infrastructure needs identified by the NIC is not going to be easy.

And in the meantime the private water companies own enormous swathes of our countryside. United Utilities, serving England's North-West, holds around 57,000 hectares of upland countryside. Yorkshire Water has about 28,000 ha, Severn Trent about 20,000 ha and Northumbrian Water (which is currently owned by a Hong Kong based holding company) about 8,500 ha. Unlike, say, the rail privatisation model where franchise holders were given time-limited licences to run services, the actual ownership of the water catchment lands was passed into private hands at privatisation. Given land value inflation since 1989, these landholdings may yet turn out to be the most valuable assets that these companies have to offer their investors.

CHAPTER 17

WESTGATE

Quarrying and mining

There is a little less to Weardale than there was once upon a time. For centuries humans have done all they can to remove the wealth that has been hidden beneath the surface of the countryside here. Holes have been dug and the stone and minerals within taken away. Weardale is one of those places where human industry and the countryside collide.

And when it comes to holes in the ground, nothing is quite as dramatic as the great cavernous void that is Heights Quarry, a little way north of the river Wear between Westgate and Eastgate. The campsite at Westgate was to be my destination for the evening and my route there took me from Edmundbyers through Rookhope and then along the footpath which skirts the eastern and southern perimeter of the quarry. Behind the protective barbed wire beside my footpath was an alien landscape that stretched as far as the eye could see, bare grey rock.

Heights is a long established feature in this part of Weardale, a limestone quarry which occupies a total of 72 hectares of ground and which has planning permission to operate until 2046, by which time six million further tonnes or so of stone should have been removed and taken away on the trucks which shuttle backwards and forwards on the private roadway which connects the quarry with the main road below. The quarry's operator is a firm called Aggregate Industries UK which is one of the largest suppliers of construction and building material in Britain, and which is owned in turn by a Swiss-based multinational called Holcim. The limestone which is obtained at Heights is crushed in a processing plant on the site and then used either as an aggregate in concrete manufacture or as road-stone, much of it coated as asphalt (that can be done on the site, too). First of all, though, the soil and overburden (the material above the rock that can't be exploited economically) has to be stripped bare and the exposed rock blasted, in a way which tries to fragment the rock as much as possible. All being well, about 250,000 tonnes of crushed limestone should be trucked away from the quarry every year for the next two decades. The vagaries of geology being what they are, Heights Quarry also produces a much smaller amount of sandstone.

How do we feel about this extremely visible intrusion of economic activity into the landscape? Do we quietly tut-tut as we peer at the heavy earth-moving equipment down on the quarry's floor? This part of Weardale is, after all, within the designated North Pennines Area of Outstanding Natural Beauty, or rather (since AONBs have recently been renamed) within one of our 'National Landscapes'. These are special places which have to be looked after. The Countryside and Rights of Way Act 2000, for example, has a requirement that public authorities have to seek to conserve and enhance the natural beauty of designated AONBs/National Landscapes.

So tut-tutting is a very natural reaction. But let's ponder this a little more. Firstly, we need to find building materials from somewhere, if the country's housing shortage is to be tackled and other new buildings put up. We need to try to provide smooth surfaces for our roads and highways free from potholes (and certainly when I am cycling I like to be able to do so on roads which are well-surfaced). So where do we look to source this raw material? Shipping it in from abroad means expending unnecessary energy on the transportation process and may mean using material obtained through exploitative working practices.

So there are benefits to somewhere like Heights Quarry. In fact, weighing up the benefits as against the downsides was exactly what Durham County councillors had to do in June 2019, when a planning application from Aggregate Industries came before the planning committee asking for Heights Quarry to be extended. The company wanted to take an extra 12 hectares of land into the quarry area, extending it from the previous 60 ha up to 72 ha. It also wanted the quarry's working life to be extended by four years, from 2042 to 2046.

The committee heard from both sides, a local resident representing the Wear Rivers Trust who was objecting, and a representative of the company making the application who was of course speaking in favour. The councillors also had before them a fifty-one page report prepared by a senior planning officer, which, paragraph by paragraph, went through the issues: soil stripping and storage, working hours, local employment, traffic implications, environmental implications, the need to divert a right of way, biodiversity, noise, heritage, hydrology, potential loss of habitat for waders, and much more, not least the fact that the quarry's location was within the North Pennines AONB. The report eventually reached its conclusion: "While the proposal would cause a degree of localised harm to the landscape of the AONB it is considered that the benefits of the proposal, in terms of crushed rock aggregate supply, jobs and future biodiversity enhancement are sufficient to outweigh this harm..." The officer's report recommended approval of the application, subject to a number of conditions. The councillors at their meeting debated the case and then voted to agree with him.

This is the way that our planning process currently operates, a quasi-judicial process which is designed at least in theory to examine the pros and cons of each planning application dispassionately, which is based on an assessment by a planning professional, which involves local councillors who have been democratically elected, and which takes place in public. The introduction of a planning system, of which the landmark legislation was the Town and Country Planning Act of 1947, was certainly a step away from the planning free-for-all which had historically existed and which among things had seen unchecked urban sprawl into the countryside in the 1920s and 1930s. Without planning controls our countryside and our cities today would be chaotic places.

And yet I'm aware that the current way that planning applications are dealt with is not one which is universally loved. The process can feel disempowering for individuals and communities who sense that those with money and influence have the opportunity to use the planning regime much more effectively than they do. The early stages of the planning process, where developers have informal pre-application discussions with planning departments, tend to take place below the radar. It's perhaps not surprising that communities come together to campaign against proposals far more frequently than they unite to support them. It's also true that those making applications have the right to appeal if councils reject their proposal but that there is no comparable right for objectors to appeal if applications are approved. What should be done to address the apparent power imbalance, that sense of community disempowerment, which seems implicit in the process?

Changes in planning procedures are definitely under discussion at the moment, but not necessarily ones to tackle this issue. Politicians have their own rather different problems with the system. In recent years governments have fretted that the planning process is simply too drawn out, slow and expensive, particularly when it comes to developments which are deemed to be nationally necessary to be progressed at speed. The shortage of new houses is one example. The new reservoirs which the National Infrastructure Commission say are urgently needed would be another. These sorts of developments may very well not be popular in the areas where they're planned to be sited, but what's the answer? Should we as a society accept shorter planning procedures so that national projects can be progressed?

In fact central government already intervenes to a considerable extent in the way that planning happens. Those Durham county councillors for example were quite tightly bound in what they could decide when they discussed Heights Quarry, because they were required to pay due attention to the National Planning Policy Framework (NPPF) and the various planning guidance notes which have been issued from Whitehall. The NPPF indeed includes a detailed section on what it calls "facilitating the sustainable use of minerals". The section begins by stating firmly: "It is essential that there is a sufficient supply of minerals to provide the infrastructure, buildings, energy and goods that the country needs. Since minerals are a finite natural resource, and can only be worked where they are found, best use needs to be made of them to secure their long-term conservation."

There's more: "When determining planning applications, great weight should be given to the benefits of mineral extraction, including to the economy". Admittedly the NPPF does advise that mineral extraction should be avoided in national parks and Areas of Outstanding Natural Beauty although it adds the rider "as far as possible". It's fair to say that an application for a brand-new limestone quarry in Weardale would probably be turned down. Heights Quarry by contrast has had planning consent to operate since the early 1960s.

There's one more important provision in the NPPF when it comes to mineral extraction, and that's the requirement that worked land is reclaimed and restored as soon as possible once the site is no longer operating. There are lengthy conditions in the Heights Quarry planning consent on what has to happen afterwards. Come back if you can in the years after 2046 and the great Heights hole is likely to look very different.

So much rearrangement of the landscapes of Weardale and its tributary valley of Rookhope Burn to the north has occurred in the cause of mineral extraction, most of it many long years before there was any suggestion of a need for planning. It's impossible if you walk this way not to be aware of this industrial legacy. My route into the village of Rookhope, for example, was down the 1 in 6 Bolt's Law incline which was originally built by the Weardale Iron and Coal Company in the 1840s as part of an extensive network of mineral railways built across the moors. The aim here was to take iron ore away to the furnaces at Tow Law and to bring coal back. The incline was built to a standard railway gauge but no locomotive then (or now) could drag wagons up such a steep incline so a stationary steam engine was installed instead to pull the wagons up by rope.

I stayed on the former extensive mineral railway network after leaving Rookhope, as I made my way past Heights Quarry towards Westgate. The Weardale Iron and Coal Company was responsible for this stretch of track too.

However it was not ironstone or coal which were historically the main things being harvested from under the hills of Weardale – it was lead.

It's easy to forget that lead mining traditionally was a major economic activity in several areas of the upland Pennines. In the North Pennines mining was focused on upper Weardale, upper Teesdale, the South Tyne valley near Alston, the two Allendales (east and west) and the Derwent valley. Elsewhere there were significant lead mining areas in the Yorkshire Dales in Swaledale, Arkengarthdale and upper Wensleydale and further south near Grassington. There was also lead mining activity in the Peak District, from the High Peak down to Ashbourne.

This lead mining history goes back a very long way. The Romans exploited the lead deposits in the Yorkshire Dales and Peak District (we know, because several pigs of lead with Roman inscriptions have been found), and they perhaps also used the deposits in Weardale and the neighbouring valleys. Among other things the Romans needed the lead for the plumbing of their bath houses. Lead was used in mediaeval times for protecting the roofs of castles and monasteries. Then, in modern times, small-scale mining was mechanised and powerful large mining companies emerged. Capitalism arrived, you might say.

Over on the Cumberland side of the North Pennines the big player was the London Lead Company, formed in 1692 and for much of its life a venture with strong Quaker roots. In Weardale by contrast most of the lead mining and smelting was in the hands of a powerful landowning family, initially the Blacketts and then (following an eighteenth century marriage of one of the Blacketts) the Beaumont family. Lead proved a very valuable business for them. The Beaumonts had their own stately home at Bywell Hall in the Tyne valley which they extensively redeveloped during the nineteenth century, and indeed the family remains there to this day, the current occupant being Wentworth Beaumont, the 4th Viscount Allendale.

Lead ore is found in mineral veins which once upon a very long time ago were mineralised streams of fluid which flowed into cracks and fissures in the limestone rock. The mineral veins are normally more or less vertical (occasionally horizontal veins can be found) and they like doing their own thing, following their own chosen routes as and how they please between their limestone walls. This makes the miner's task of finding them and then removing the ore a skilful one. It's a completely different approach to that of mining coal deposits.

In early days the ore was simply taken from deposits near the surface, shafts being dug down following the line of the veins. But from the eighteenth century the construction of 'levels' began to become much more common. Levels are slightly sloping but broadly horizontal tunnels dug into the side of a hill from lower down a hillside, designed to meet up with shafts dug down from the top. Levels are a way of draining water from the bottom of a mine and they also help provide ventilation. An additional advantage is that you can dig up from a level into ore-bearing veins which can be easier than having to dig down to obtain the ore.

There are old levels to be found all over the lead mining areas of the North Pennines, often with elaborate stone portals where they emerge from the gloom of the hillside into daylight. Later levels were built high and wide enough to be able to accommodate horses who could then pull out the 'bouse' (the mixture of ore and rock taken by the miners) on wagons running on roughly-laid railway tracks. Levels could extend for several miles underground and they helped transform the industry, but they also required extensive capital outlay for no immediate result. They needed much deeper pockets than the lead miners themselves were likely to possess.

So what about the life of a miner? Arthur Raistrick, the Yorkshire geologist and historian who was one of the first to research the story of Pennine lead mining, once put it like this: "In every way water was the miners' common enemy. He would as often as not arrive at the mine wet or at least wetshod; he might change into mine clothes at the 'shop' but at the smaller mines his clothes would be cold and damp and plastered with clay. Underground, water would be dripping from the roof, running on the level floors and in deeper workings threatening always to drown him out and sometimes succeeding."

Raistrick goes on to say that water was only one of the issues: "Ventilation was always a difficult problem. A level driven far into the hillside or a drift taken from the bottom of a shaft was a dead end, and little fresh air could enter except with some mechanical help. The heavy breathing of the miner, the burning of his candle and often the fumes of gunpowder combined to keep the air foul..."

If a damp atmosphere made for an unhealthy workplace a very dry atmosphere was if anything worse, especially when power drills and dynamite started being used in the later nineteenth century. Lead miners notoriously suffered from lung complaints, mainly silicosis and other forms of pneumoconiosis, brought about from scars on the lungs caused by inhaling mineral dust. Among other things this left them very vulnerable to catching TB. Their life expectancy was shockingly low. According to Christopher Hunt, the author of the 1970 book *The Lead Miners of the North Pennines*, life expectancy in 1832 was 45. Hunt also suggests that this was actually an improvement: the average life expectancy in the eighteenth century could have been as low as 35, he says.

The miners were traditionally independent workers rather than employees of the lead mining firms, striking 'bargains' with the companies to work particular mines and being paid not on the hours worked but on the quantity of ore removed. In reality power was always more with the company than the miner and during the nineteenth century the idea that lead mining could be based on some form of business relationship between two contracting parties was stretched to breaking point, with the Beaumont mine agent in Weardale Thomas Sopwith pushing for factory-style working arrangements with regular working hours and the clocking in and out of shifts. There was at least one significant strike in Weardale as miners tried to resist these changes. However, in Christopher Hunt's words, "the sub-contractors were direct employees in all but name". Today we talk of the gig economy where taxi drivers and fast food delivery workers purportedly work as independent contractors to the digital platforms that give them their work. It turns out that the Weardale miners lived with their own version of the gig economy two centuries ago.

Boys from about the age of nine had work to do too, not initially underground but outside on the moors at the entrances to the mines on what were known as the washing floors or dressing floors (women also were sometimes put to work here). Their task was to use hammers to break down the rock and ore coming out of the ground into small pieces about the size of fine gravel so that the ore could more easily be separated from the waste material. A commissioner visiting the North Pennines in 1842 for the government's Children's Employment Commission reported on the almost complete lack of protection from the weather for workers on the washing floors. If it rained (and rain in the Pennines is not unheard of) you got wet and stayed wet.

The washing floors have gone and with them the washer lads who worked them, but what has survived is a song about their work. *Fourpence a Day* was collected by Ewan MacColl and Joan Littlewood in 1949 from the singing of a retired lead miner but the song itself is attributed to the earlier miner and working-class poet Thomas Raine, who it is said originally came from Barnard Castle. It has been widely anthologised and recorded and, as you would expect from a folk song, can be found in different variants. Here's how the first verse of one version begins:

> *The ore is waiting in the tubs, the snow's upon the fells;*
> *Canny folk are sleeping yet, but lead is reet to sell*
> *Come, my little washer lad, come let's away,*
> *We're bound down to slavery for fourpence a day.*

I said at the start of this chapter that there was less to Weardale these days than there had been once, and what the valley has lost is not limited just to what used to lie beneath the soil. The valley has also lost many of its people. The volunteer-run community museum of Weardale life in Ireshopeburn has collections of evocative photos of the days when lead mining was thriving, and I absent-mindedly leafed through the album for Rookhope. There was one photo of the village's primary school which particularly caught my eye. It showed the playground simply filled to bursting with children. And now? In February 2024 the BBC website ran a news story with the headline *Remote school with five pupils to permanently close*. Durham County Council had just announced that Rookhope primary school would close at the end of the school year: it had been saved once before in 2016 when there were twenty children on the roll but, as the council pointed out, there had simply been no children for several years coming in as new pupils to the Reception year class. Rookhope's pub recently closed as well, a victim of the covid pandemic. I'm pleased to say that the small village shop just round the corner which doubles up as a post office was still there as I passed through, although only open in the mornings. (I bought some snacks to try to support it.) But that photo album tells of such a different world, one gone for good.

There had been economic downturns for the lead mining firms at various times during the nineteenth century and miners and their families had sometimes left in large numbers. However the industry went into what was an almost terminal decline in the late 1870s and early 1880s, a time when foreign lead was being imported at prices which local producers could not match. The number of miners needed for the remaining operations fell rapidly, and emigration had probably never seemed so attractive. The museum in Ireshopeburn tells the story of the sailing ship Margaret Galbraith which left London in the Autumn of 1879 for the long voyage to New Zealand's South Island. Of the 149 passengers on board, about sixty came from the two tiny Weardale settlements of Killhope and Cowshill. Somehow one hopes that their new lives in New Zealand were easier and kinder than the lives they had left behind.

Killhope is about as far as you can go before the river Wear reduces to a trickle and Durham gives way to Cumberland, and it is here that an attempt is being made today to try to remember the history of lead mining in the valley. The Killhope Museum has been run by the county council since 1980 on the site of the former Killhope mine and although it was temporarily closed for refurbishment its manager Maria McArdle arranged for me to make a visit. I was given, as you might say, the inside story of the mine, for (suitably kitted out in wellies and a miner's helmet) I was taken by two of Maria's colleagues for a few hundred yards inside the former Park level to see for myself how things look from within a damp North Pennine hillside. The trip into the level has traditionally been one of the highlights of the visitor experience at Killhope, albeit the part open to the public is only the beginning of what were once several miles of level (it's also only fair to say that some of what you get to see is a very convincing reconstruction rather than the original mine workings).

In addition to the level, Killhope Museum still has its large nineteenth-century waterwheel in situ, the lodging shop where miners living at a

The Pennine Way, Britain's first 'long distance trail'

Hadrian's Wall and the Mithras Temple. Below, the car park at Brocolitia on Hadrian's Wall

The author at Hexham Abbey. Below, the countryside south of Hexham

Blanchland estate village and (below) what a grouse moor with an efficient gamekeeper can look like

Lupins in
Weardale. Below,
Heights Quarry

The River Tees at Low Force. Below, may blossom in Teesdale

The old station at Romaldkirk (complete with relocated signal).
Below, Barnard Castle and the Tees

Above: Military ranges
near Richmond.

Below: warriors past and present
- sculpture at Catterick Bridge.
Right: Journey's End - the Swale as
viewed from Catterick Bridge.

distance from Killhope would have boarded between weekends (and would have run the real risk of catching TB from fellow miners in the process), and a reconstruction of the washing floor. This, according to Maria, is one of the highlights of many children's visits to Killhope, because here they are given the opportunity to bash away at bouse and rock with little hammers. "We're a hands-on museum," Maria says.

Once young children spent their days here, quite often soaking wet, to earn their fourpence a day. Now it's a visitor attraction. I think that has to be counted as some form of progress.

CHAPTER 18

SWINHOPE HEAD

Peat

Where might you think would be the highest ground I would cross on my journey south from Edinburgh? Scald Law in the Pentland Hills is obviously a contender, but the border on the Cheviots where Dere Street meets the Pennine Way somehow seems more likely.

Both wrong. The answer is a nondescript summit with the name of Swinhope Head on the bleak ridge of moorland that separates Weardale from upper Teesdale, which my Ordnance Survey map tells me is 607 metres above sea-level. Up here is high ground that has been hard-worked for its minerals in the past, where – who knows? – there may still be uncapped mine shafts lurking in among the tough moor grasses and where it's therefore probably best not to go wandering at will when the mist is down and visibility is limited.

The mist was down and visibility was limited when I reached Swinhope Head. Admittedly, the route there from my campsite at Westgate had been straightforward enough, just up the little gated country road which, had I stayed on it, ultimately would have taken me over to Newbiggin in Teesdale.

But at Swinhope Head I had decided to leave the road behind and make my way south-westwards across open country to reach the Tees a little further upstream from Newbiggin, near Low Force waterfall. The map suggested that the way would be pretty rough walking, but reassuringly there was a footpath marked that I planned to follow. Indeed, even better, the path was flagged up on the map as part of a long-distance route named A Pennine Journey.

It was shortly after the formation in 2002 of the Wainwright Society, a group which aims to keep Alfred Wainwright's legacy alive and to maintain his fell-walking traditions, that two keen long distance walkers David and Heather Pitt suggested to the Society that his *A Pennine Journey* book could be suitably remembered by creating a long-distance trail based on his route. The idea was taken up, the route was finalised and a guidebook to it edited by David and Heather was first published in 2010. The trail is now looked after by a separate organisation with its own website, the Pennine Journey Supporters Club.

Wainwright reached this part of the North Pennines on his fourth day of walking from Settle and he made his way over Swinhope Head in weather similar to mine. "As I got higher into the hills and saw my way rising over a bleak moorland and into mist I knew that once again I was to be made wet," he wrote. "On this occasion the mist was so dense and its lower limit so well defined that the hill appeared to be beheaded. I approached a white wall which seemed as solid and immoveable as a cliff; it did not drift down to meet me, but sternly awaited." Still, Wainwright seemed to be in good heart. There was, he maintained, "an invigorating quality about rain". He stopped at Swinhope Head in the shelter of a wall and lit himself a cigarette.

It's fairly clear from his account that Wainwright had taken the more obvious option from Teesdale into Weardale, straight up the country road from Newbiggin to Westgate, but I understand why the group who planned the Pennine Journey trail diverted a little from his exact route. In 1938 country roads were quiet affairs with few cars. Today too many roads in the countryside are too busy with traffic for walkers to feel comfortable on them. Diverting from the original route when Wainwright followed roads on to nearby footpaths would seem to make good sense.

Except that in the case of the route chosen between Swinhope Head and the Tees valley near Low Force the path – very clear on the map – is anything but very clear on the ground. I was anticipating waymarks to help me, similar perhaps to the way that the Cross Borders Drove Road had waymarked my route through the Scottish borderlands north of Selkirk, but I think that almost all the waymarks that once may have been here have long since been swallowed up in peat bogs (or perhaps fallen down mine shafts). Leaving Swinhope Head behind means compass-work, bashing your way through the tussocks and hoping for the best.

To be fair to the Pennine Journey Supporters Club, they are aware of the difficulties on this stretch of their route and their website advises walkers to follow Wainwright's lead and use the Newbiggin to Westgate road instead when the weather is poor. But I do wonder whether Ordnance Survey should have marked this particular path quite so prominently.

I mentioned peat bogs a moment ago. My walk between Weardale and Teesdale was not only taking me to the highest ground I would encounter, it was also taking me over some of the deepest peat I would be walking on. And peat, as you will already have appreciated from earlier chapters, is really something very important.

Anyone who walks in the uplands of Britain will be familiar with blanket bogs, so-called because the peat forms a blanket across the underlying terrain. The peat can be deep, as much as six metres in depth and occasionally even deeper, and if I mention that new peat accumulates at a rate of no more than two millimetres a year and quite often at less than a single millimetre a year you will appreciate that what we have beneath our feet in areas like the North Pennine moors is the result of what has happened over millennia. In fact, Britain's blanket bogs began very slowly accumulating shortly after glaciers had left our shores about ten thousand years ago.

Britain has plenty of peatland, around 3 million hectares in total or about 12% of our total land area. Indeed we have more than you might expect, for peatlands contribute only about 3% to the world's land mass. England itself holds about 1.4 million hectares. Some of these are the areas of lowland peat, for example in the Fens, but most of the country's peat is up on the high ground, in blanket bogs. If you are interested, you will find brightly coloured maps of the locations of all our peatlands online, produced by Natural England and its Scottish and Welsh equivalent bodies NatureScot and Natural Resources Wales.

Peat is caused because waterlogging has prevented plants when they die from properly decomposing. Normally when plants decay the carbon held by the plant is released back into the atmosphere. But if ground is very wet the lack of oxygen can prevent micro-organisms from getting to work and the process of decomposition doesn't happen. Dead plants are instead slowly turned into peat, with the carbon retained in the soil.

For upland blanket bogs to be created, plenty of rainfall is needed to create the right watery conditions. Scientists researching this topic have suggested that about 160 wet days year is the minimum, with about 1,000-1,200 millimetres of rain falling in the course of a year a further requirement. Average summer temperatures shouldn't be too high (a mean of less than 15° C is suggested) and there shouldn't be major seasonal fluctuations in the climate, either.

Meet these conditions and you have the potential to make a really healthy peat bog. How do you tell if a bog is healthy? It will be lovely and gloopy, with plenty of sphagnum mosses and other specialist moorland vegetation – plants like hare's-tail cotton grass, bog myrtle and the round-leaved sundew (a carnivorous plant, taking nutrients from insects). Little berry-bearing mountain shrubs should also be there, including plants such as the cranberry, cowberry and bearberry.

You'll also recognise a healthy blanket bog if you find yourself falling into one. I've met a few in my time: there was the one, for example, several years ago up near Cold Fell in the North Pennines which caught me by surprise and gobbled me up to my waist before I realised what was happening and, with some difficulty, managed to extricate myself. (The comprehensive 200-page guide for ecologists *Conserving Bogs: the Management Handbook* warns at one stage that "bogs can be dangerous places". The handbook goes on to claim that the preserved body of a man still mounted on horseback was found in a bog a few miles south of Falkirk, a good story but one which my best journalistic efforts to check out have failed to corroborate. Nevertheless, many human bodies – and not just Pete Marsh, the name given to a body found in a Cheshire bog – have been found preserved in peat.)

Unfortunately, though, healthy bogs have become increasingly hard to find. The vast majority of Britain's peatland is in very poor condition. In fact, surveys have found that only about 22% of our peatlands are in what could be described as near-natural conditions. The rest have been degraded through human intervention in the landscape.

This intervention takes and has taken many forms. We've already seen how the demands of the grouse shooting estates have encouraged regular moorland burning and with it the establishment of dry moorlands with heather monoculture. Another factor has been the decision to create new commercial forests on peatland. The issue here is that the process of getting the ground ready for trees to be planted usually involves both draining of the land and major disturbance of the soil.

Industrialisation has had its effect on our blanket bogs too, especially in the South Pennines and Peak District which were downwind from the sulphur-emitting chimneys of the mills of Lancashire and Yorkshire and the coal fires of their workers' houses. As a consequence over many decades the peatland suffered severe acidification ('like the acid in a car battery', I was once told). The land also became contaminated with pollutants such as lead. Although things have improved markedly since the middle of the last century, the legacy of all this industrial activity continues to affect the health of these moorlands today.

Public policy in the last century also deliberately tried to encourage the drying of blanket bog terrain. There were generous government subsidies available to landowners who wanted to dry out their boggy peatlands by digging drainage channels (these channels are known as moorland grips, the process being referred to as gripping). Now, a generation or two on, there are subsidies available to undertake the work to try to block these grips in order to rewet the peatlands. They do say (though this may be apocryphal) that some of the same contractors who got money to create the grips in the first place are now being paid for the opportunity to block them up.

Indeed, generally public policy towards upland agriculture after the Second World War contributed to the degradation of blanket bogs. Farmers were encouraged to maximise food production and this meant that unsustainable levels of livestock were left to graze on the upland moors, preventing the regeneration of vegetation. Put too many sheep on the high ground and you'll find that they are feasting on the succulent young shoots of the plants which should be growing for the future.

Whatever the causes, our blanket bogs have been allowed to dry out. At its worst a degraded blanket bog will be left with completely bare peat, the sort of landscape which was (and still is, to an extent) a familiar part of areas of the Peak District such as Kinder Scout and Bleaklow with their deep bare peat channels known as groughs. Other dry moorlands may have bare patches of peat interspersed with some grassy vegetation (the plants that the sheep reject, in particular hardy plants like molinia – purple moor grass – remain and create the tussocks that are probably the least favourite feature of moorland landscapes for walkers).

In addition to the lack of biodiversity, dried-out peatland increases the risk of flash flooding off the land and discolouration of drinking water, two issues I mentioned briefly in relation to grouse moors. But the overriding issue, the one which has drawn so many researchers into this area of study in recent years, is the effect it has on global warming.

Peat is an extremely good store of carbon, sequestrating the carbon which, were plants to have decayed in the usual way, would have been lost into the atmosphere. In fact, peat does an altogether better job of storing carbon than do trees. Taking a global view, there's more carbon locked worldwide in peat than in trees, perhaps twice as much. Forests are important, but bogs are even more important.

For century after century peat accumulation took place and the carbon within the peat also increased. But in recent times as it has been allowed to dry out peat has started to release the carbon it holds: it has become, to use the terminology, a carbon source rather than a carbon sink. Researchers have undertaken detailed studies which suggest that in total UK peatlands are releasing 23 million tons of carbon dioxide equivalent each year (that's 23,000,000 tCO_2e yr-1, to utilise the formula I briefly introduced earlier). Some carbon escapes directly into the atmosphere while some is carried away in water, either dissolved or in the form of particulates.

There's still a great deal of carbon left in our peat (around 3.2 billion tonnes in total, it's been said) but nevertheless at a time when the UK government has formally committed to reduce greenhouse gas emissions any release of stored carbon from peat is worrying. Since the issue began to receive proper attention, at the end of the last century and the start of the current one, considerable efforts have been made to try to restore blanket bogs. Funding has come in large part from public sources (including, while we had the opportunity to draw it down, from the European Union through its environment and climate funding stream known as the LIFE programme). The UK National Committee of the International Union for Conservation of Nature (IUCN) has played a key role in developing awareness about peat restoration and there have been important projects on the ground such as Moors for the Future, which originally began its work on the most barren areas of the Peak District.

The North Pennines has seen activity too, until recently in a major initiative partly made possible through a LIFE-funded project, and those involved have recently teamed up with Moors for the Future and other peat restoration organisations in the North of England in a partnership to which they've given the name of the Great North Bog. Someone involved in this venture has managed to come up with a memorable name.

There have also been initiatives in Scotland, including those undertaken through the programme called Peatland ACTION which is backed by the Scottish government and is run under the auspices of NatureScot. In total Peatland ACTION claims to have improved about 45,000 hectares of degraded peat in the years since 2012, with the target being to have tackled a total of 250,000 ha by the end of this decade. Peat restoration projects in England have more than matched Scotland's efforts, although we have a very long way to go before we get anywhere close to the 2m+ hectares of peat north and south of the border which are in need of some TLC. Even with all the efforts being taken our blanket bogs are still currently net sources of carbon rather than carbon sinks.

However there is now plenty of experience to draw on in terms of how to get your patch of peat properly restored. Each area of blanket bog is different, of course, but generally the aim of a restoration programme is to try to rewet the land and raise the water table. To achieve this is typically likely to involve as an initial step the blocking of grips and water channels by creating 'leaky dams' made from wood, bales of heather, coconut fibre, stone or even peat itself. Steep slopes of bare peat may be flattened out a little to enable vegetation to grow more easily.

The ground being treated will then very often be covered with heather brash (cut heather) to prevent the soil underneath from being eroded, to keep the moisture in, and to encourage the germination of seeds. Very large canvas bags of cut brash, probably delivered by helicopter, can sometimes be seen lined up on moorlands, waiting their turn to be spread. A friend of mine, seeing several bags lying apparently abandoned in the countryside, complained that the fly-tippers had been busy. But no, it's not fly-tipping: it's all part of the plan.

The key objective is to get sphagnum mosses to colonise the peat, sphagnum being extremely good at absorbing and holding water and therefore very good at helping encourage the process of peat accumulation. The peat restoration efforts in the North Pennines have been trying several approaches, including spreading pellets of clay-coated sphagnum spores, using plugs of the plants specially grown by nurseries, and also taking clumps of the moss from healthy blanket bogs and planting these by hand in the new areas. Whichever approach you take involves plenty of hard work on high ground where, of course, there is no guarantee that the weather will be kind to you.

But slogging your way through the rough stuff on to the high ground is only one part of the picture. Paul Leadbitter has been the manager in charge of peat restoration work in the North Pennines for many years now and says that increasingly he and his team are reliant on technology to assist them. Computer modelling based on GIS (geographic information system) data can advise them on the best way to approach restoration work on particular sites: where best to put in the dams, for example, to restore moorland hydrology. He adds that drones, or as they are officially called unmanned aerial vehicles (UAVs), are becoming more and more important for assessing restoration projects. "UAVs have become like a hammer is to a carpenter, you have to have them. We're using quadcopters now, which are much more effective than fixed-wing drones. The cameras are much better, too," he says.

Fortunately the peatland in the North Pennines which these UAVs are sizing up ready for restoration planning doesn't replicate the great expanses of bare eroded ground which can be found further south. "Our damage is more like freckles on the landscape, bald bits surrounded by better bits," Paul says. Nevertheless removing those freckles will not happen overnight. There are several thousand damaged areas of peat which have been identified in the North Pennines which ideally need attention.

As it turns out, the most damaged peatland in the whole North Pennines area according to Paul is that expanse of high ground between Weardale and upper Teesdale – exactly the watershed country which I found myself traversing on my way down towards Low Force. A start, at least, has been made here: a restoration project at Valance Lodge, a 96 hectare site south-west of Swinhope Head, has recently been completed with the help of about 1,200 tonnes of stone for damming the grips and about 90,000 clumps of harvested sphagnum moss for the newly rewetted peat.

Restoring degraded peat is a long-term business. Academic research suggests that it can take forty years before a peat bog is fully back to health and is converted into being a carbon sink again. Nevertheless there are shorter-term benefits. What's important is not that carbon is being immediately sequestrated but rather that less of the carbon which is already in the peat is eroding away.

There's one danger to try to guard against and that is the unhelpful possibility that methane (marsh gas) may be naturally generated in new swamps and pools of water. Methane as we've seen is another greenhouse gas, one which is a more potent gas than carbon although fortunately much shorter-lived. Risking the creation of new methane for the atmosphere as a side-effect of peat restoration is clearly not desirable but the message from the experts is that the benefits of restoration are worth the risk.

Paul Leadbitter talks of the preparatory work that has to take place before a new peatland project gets under way. These include the requirement to get landowner permission, the biosecurity issues to address and the consents needed to work on moorland hydrology and watercourses. But perhaps the greatest challenge is to get the funding in place to make it happen at all.

The Valance Lodge project was able to proceed through a package of finance which included government funding (including grants from farming schemes), money from Natural England, grant-funding from the National Lottery Heritage Fund and (just in time, before Brexit removed this opportunity) from the EU LIFE programme. There was also support from another source, from a private sector construction firm.

For Paul Leadbitter, the private sector has to play its part in the work he and his colleagues are trying to achieve. "We've got to sit down and have a conversation with the private sector. Rather than being apologetic about being conservationists, we have to have active dialogue," he says. Working through the Great North Bog partnership he has, he hopes, helped identify five corporates interested in participating in future restoration. Grants as part of companies' Corporate Social Responsibility agenda are a possibility. But there is also potentially the opportunity of funding for carbon offsetting.

There is in fact an established way to try to coax private sector finance into peatland restoration. In a very similar way to the Woodland Carbon Code (page 38) with its Pending Issuance Units (PIUs) and Woodland Carbon Units (WCUs) there is now a Peatland Code providing an accreditation procedure for companies and organisations wanting to buy into the voluntary carbon sequestration market via peat restoration. The Peatland Code, overseen by the IUNC UK Peatland Programme, provides for peatland PIUs and (once certified) Peatland Carbon Units. As with approved forestry initiatives, approved Peatland Code projects are listed on the publicly available UK Land Carbon Registry. Projects have to continue for at least thirty years, with peatland managed in a restored condition for the whole period. Basically to get your Peatland Carbon Units you have to demonstrate that carbon which would have escaped from peat has really been reduced.

"Private finance will be vital if we are to meet our restoration ambitions," the then-Conservative government stated firmly in its *English Peat Action Plan*, produced in 2021. We are back in the world of finding ways to put monetary values on 'natural capital'. And perhaps, or so the government's report suggested enthusiastically, there may be other future possibilities. What about creating a market in 'habitat banking', for example? Undertake work to help increase biodiversity in areas of peatland which haven't yet been considered important enough to be designated as SSSIs and maybe this could enable you to create a market to buy and sell 'Biodiversity Units'. "We shall look… to monetise all of the potential ecosystem services provided by peatland restoration, in all settings," the report concluded.

Paul Leadbitter is aware that the process of drawing in the private sector may be complicated and protracted but he still hopes that companies will take the issue of peat loss seriously: "We have a biodiversity crisis, we have a climate change crisis. We haven't got a lot of time left to try to get some of these things done. People who run companies have children and grandchildren…. Surely they're interested?"

CHAPTER 19

LOW FORCE

Long distance walking

I'd left the Pennine Way many miles earlier, a little to the south of the town of Bellingham. Now, just the other side of the Tees after I'd crossed on the two-hundred year old Wynch suspension bridge, I met it again. While I had been making my way down through Weardale, the Pennine Way had made a sashay west to traverse the tops of Cross Fell and Great Dun Fell before heading back eastwards again towards me.

We reunited just below Low Force, one of the two major falls on this stretch of the Tees, the other (a little further upstream) being the even more impressive waterfall that, logically enough, bears the name High Force. The water may be forceful as it tumbles over the rocks but the name is straightforwardly Viking, a slight Anglifying of the Scandinavian word for waterfall, *foss.*

For several miles here the Pennine Way follows the upper Tees valley, eschewing the high moorlands for lush riverside meadows. Alfred Wainwright was delighted by this part of the route, calling the path immediately south of Low Force "the most beautiful" mile of all in his *Pennine Way Companion,* first published in 1968. "This is a place to linger, to rest awhile in sylvan sweetness and dream. It is the river, the Tees, with its bordering carpet of flowers, that enchants the eye and uplifts the heart," he wrote. It should probably be added that he had encountered pretty poor weather elsewhere when he was researching his Pennine Way book. In any case I think we can deduce that he was rather fonder of his beloved Lake District fells than he seems to have been of the Pennine moorlands.

The Pennine Way has achieved some sort of iconic status as the originator of all Britain's long-distance trails, with something of a reputation for being a tough and gruelling undertaking. It's a reputation that is not entirely undeserved. In the course of the 268 miles (give or take) between Edale and Kirk Yetholm walkers face some 36,000 feet of climbing and some of the most remote countryside which England has to offer. The pastoral section along the Tees valley is unusual: normally the Pennine Way prefers to seek out the isolated places. Kinder Scout, Bleaklow, Black Hill, Pen-y-ghent, Great Shunner Fell, Cross Fell, the Cheviots – the list of places en route is a roll-call of some of the country's remoter hill country.

Perhaps it's not quite as hard work as it may have been in the early days. The paving (often using old paving slabs from mills) of what were once particularly wet sections of the route has been undertaken, not primarily to make it easier for walkers but to try to combat the erosion from which the path was suffering. The peat restoration work undertaken in recent years in the Peak District and South Pennines has also made a significant difference to both the landscape and the walking experience. Take Black Hill in the southern Pennines, for example. Wainwright when he came here railed against the 'sea of ooze' which he found waiting for him: "Nothing can grow in this acid waste," he wrote. "It is a frightening place in bad weather, a dangerous place after heavy rain. It is NOT a place to visit unaccompanied, especially after prolonged rainy weather, because of the risk of becoming trapped or even entombed in the seepage hollows..."

In fact, the peat restoration carried out by the Moors for the Future team over a number of years in the early part of this century has demonstrated conclusively that vegetation cover is possible even on the Black Hill peat. Wainwright thought the hill's name all too appropriate, given the conditions he found there. Now it is rather less apposite. The peatland of Black Hill has been successfully turning green.

The Pennine Way's status as the first of Britain's long-distance trails is not to be gainsaid, however. As with the early campaigning for national parks this was an idea inspired by what was happening elsewhere in the world, and in particular in the United States. The proposal for a very long walking route the length of the Appalachian Mountains in eastern USA between Georgia and Maine was first made in 1921 and the Appalachian Trail was completed (all 2,200 miles of it) in 1937. A similar idea in California led to the John Muir Trail (a rather more modest 213 miles) which was created between 1915 and 1938.

It was the Appalachian Trail which was referenced by Tom Stephenson in a feature article he wrote in the *Daily Herald* in June 1935, advocating something similar in Britain – advocating, in fact, what he calls in his article "a Pennine Way from the Peak to the Cheviots". Why not emulate the Americans?, he asked. Why not look to create a "meandering way deviating as needs be to include the best of that long range of moor and fell"? Why not create "just a faint line on the Ordnance Maps which the feet of grateful pilgrims would, with the passing years, engrave on the face of the land"?

I introduced Stephenson briefly earlier, quoting his criticism of those municipal water authorities who had tried to keep ramblers off their land. By the time he came to write his memoir *Forbidden Land* he was to have seen his Pennine 'faint line' very much turned into reality. But it was to be a long drawn-out process to get there.

Tom Stephenson was born in 1893 in Chorley in Lancashire, a working-class boy in a working-class town. His father worked in a factory where calico cloth was printed while his mother worked in a local cotton mill. He began work at thirteen, following his father's line of work by becoming an apprentice printer, but at the same time he worked hard on improving his education, attending night school and raiding local public libraries for what they could offer him. He also discovered very quickly the northern hills on his doorstep. He described later how, as a young man when work was hard to find and he had time on his hands, he would set out rambling at dawn with a little food and a few pence in his pocket and would sometimes undertake trips of at least a hundred miles before returning home. Nights would be spent bivvying inside a rolled groundsheet in the shelter of a wall or dossing down under cover in a barn. Stephenson knew the English countryside intimately from hard-won first-hand experience.

The First World War broke out when Tom was in his early twenties. He had already become politically active and he opposed the war, registering as a conscientious objector. ("Very few people agreed with my stand on the war... Of course I was the subject of a good deal of abuse," he later wrote.) He was initially (and unusually) granted absolute exemption as a CO from military service but his case was reviewed in 1917 and this time he was forcibly enlisted in the East Lancashire Regiment. Still refusing to fight, he was court-martialled and sentenced to twelve months of hard labour in Wormwood Scrubs. The opportunity which seemed to have opened up in 1915 when he had won one of only two coveted geology scholarships offered by the Royal College of Science evaporated. After the war Stephenson found work as a full-time officer with the young Labour Party and then, in the early 1930s, switched to journalism, editing a trade union magazine called *Hiker and Camper* and writing regularly for the left-of-centre *Daily Herald*.

His 1935 article proposing the creation of a long distance path along the Pennines is now considered something of a landmark moment in the story of the British outdoor movement. Wainwright in the introduction to *Pennine Way Companion* fulsomely praises the role played by Stephenson in bringing the path into being. The Pennine Way was the "happy inspiration" of Tom Stephenson, he wrote. "Officially, Whitehall created the Pennine Way. But those who walk it should remember that it was one man who inspired, in his mind and by his patience and effort, the freedom they enjoy."

The point is an important one. The Pennine Way was not an initiative dreamed up by a government ministry or an official countryside agency but rather an idea which came very much from the bottom-up and which was achieved by persistent grassroots campaigning. In fact the excitement as the idea began to be fleshed out in detail not just by Stephenson but by other key figures in the outdoor movement at the time shines through in the correspondence which has survived from the later 1930s. The letters between Stephenson (living on Clapham Common in south London) and other ramblers, most notably Edwin Royce in Manchester, have been preserved in the London Archives in the City of London. I spent a rewarding day there some time ago leafing through the folders to see how the familiar route that the Pennine Way today follows really took shape.

Here, for example, is what Royce wrote to Stephenson in November 1936: "The object is to discover where there are breaks in the chain of existing footpaths, and then to consider how to fill in these gaps. A cursory examination indicates that there are comparatively few gaps, but the links in many cases are roads, and there should be an alternative for the walker. In other cases there are paths, but not quite the Pennine Way idea." Stephenson replied to Royce a short time later: "The ideal Pennine Way I had in mind was a continuous path from the Peak to the Cheviots. From an examination of the maps, it seemed that once away from the close preserves of the Peak, it would be possible to plan an almost continuous line. This, of course, would mean a meandering route to utilise as many existing paths as possible." Stephenson recognised that making it happen might involve a degree of pragmatism, though: "Whilst it would be desirable for the track to keep to the heights and rough ground as much as possible, it would no doubt be necessary to compromise in places and to accept whatever could be attained," he added later in the same letter.

Stephenson in his *Daily Herald* article had already offered a detailed check-list of some of the potential places on the route. He had suggested the new route should begin at Edale, as of course it does, and he had also named other potential landmarks, places such as Bleaklow, Blackstone Edge, Fountains Fell, Pen-y-ghent, Hardraw, Keld, Tan Hill, and Cross Fell, all of which did indeed end up on the Pennine Way. But nevertheless he and Royce wrestled with some of the details. For a time they discussed whether the trail should be taken over Pendle Hill and towards the Forest of Bowland, before deciding that traversing the area round Burnley made the idea less attractive. Boulsworth Hill (on the Pennine chain where Yorkshire and Lancashire meet) was also pondered, as was Cold Fell at the northern end of the Pennines. Royce at one stage raised the possibility of Wild Boar Fell above Mallerstang in the northern Dales, while admitting the moors there enjoyed no existing rights of way. Both men were exercised about the issue of getting access to what Royce called "trespassers will be prosecuted country" in the Peak District between Edale and Glossop.

By the beginning of 1937 it is clear that the discussions over the potential route were bearing fruit: "I have been able to get down to the 'Pennine Way' project and now have the thing on paper in a more or less sketchy form," Royce wrote to Stephenson in January, adding that he felt the "worst bit" of the route would be the industrial mill town landscape north of Blackstone Edge with its "surfeit of mill chimneys".

By early 1938 Stephenson and Royce were ready to share their thinking more widely, and a ramblers' conference was called for the end of February at a guest house in Hope in the Peak District run by the Workers' Travel Association. It was an invitation-only event, with the 26 delegates who attended representing ramblers' federations, youth hostel groups and footpath preservation societies active at the time. Stephenson had marked up 1-inch Ordnance Survey maps between Edale and the Cheviots with a suggested route, coloured in either green or red ink – the red sections being those where existing footpaths weren't available and new legal rights of access would need to be sought.

Fortunately most of the map was green. Stephenson had calculated that the total mileage of the route was 251 miles, of which only 68 miles required new paths.

The conference (fortified by seven pounds and ten shillings' worth of refreshments donated by the *Daily Herald*) was clearly a lively affair, not without disagreement, but by the end it had resolved to establish the Pennine Way Association to progress the idea and had also established sub-committees to survey route choices in detail on the ground. "I think there is promise of the scheme becoming a live issue with a wide appeal," Stephenson wrote to a business colleague a few days later. And indeed the *Manchester Guardian* commissioned a 500-word piece from Royce on the event which it headlined with the optimistic title "250-mile Hike Will Soon be Possible".

If only. There is an entertaining exchange from May 1938 in the London archive between an enthusiastic clergyman planning a walking holiday the following week and wanting Stephenson to send him full details of the exact route of the new path that he should follow, and Stephenson's weary reply that "in reply to your enquiry the Pennine Way at the moment is an unachieved ideal".

Royce shared Stephenson's caution. He sent the *Manchester Guardian* cutting to Stephenson immediately after it had appeared, privately adding, "Personally I do not agree with its optimism, knowing some of our landowners… And I am very dubious about 'peace in our time'".

Royce was right to be sceptical on both counts. War broke out eighteen months later, and although the Pennine Way Association continued its work, and although the Hobhouse Report embraced the Pennine Way suggestion in 1947, and although Hugh Dalton, the Minister for Local Government and Planning, formally approved the Pennine Way in July 1951, and although many ramblers began unofficially tackling the route (or some version of it) in the 1950s, it was not until 1965 that the Pennine Way was formally opened. It had taken thirty years for the vision that was Stephenson's – and Royce's too – to become official.

However the Pennine Way opened the way for the development of further long-distance trails through the British countryside, a network for walkers (and more recently for off-road cyclists and horse-riders as well) which is arguably as important a part of our country's infrastructure as our roads or railways or canals. Natural England is currently in the process of completing the English Coast Path, the most ambitious of all the trails, and is also about to formally adopt the

Coast-to-Coast Walk created by Alfred Wainwright, by which time there will be seventeen 'official' long-distance trails in England and Wales. Not among the seventeen but already open and enjoyed by walkers is the complete Llwybr Arfordir Cymru/Wales Coast Path, which has been developed between Chepstow and Chester.

Scotland has taken a different route. The West Highland Way was the country's first official long-distance trail, opened in 1980, and this was joined shortly afterwards by the Speyside Way and the Southern Upland Way and (a little later) by the Great Glen Way. But NatureScot has recently broadened things out so that another 25 erstwhile unofficial routes have been embraced into what are now marketed collectively as Scotland's Great Trails. This means that my old friends the Cross Borders Drove Road and St Cuthbert's Way are on the list – and deservedly so.

This approach seems to me the right one, for it gives worthy recognition of all the voluntary efforts which have been undertaken to give us the choice we now have when we want to go walking. Stephenson and Royce's pioneering work in poring over Ordnance Survey maps in the 1930s has been replicated up and down the country since then by individuals and groups getting out maps of their own areas and seeing what routes they can devise to show off the best of their local landscapes. David and Heather Pitt whose determination it was which created the Pennine Journey trail are simply two people among many.

Some of these trails have now been accepted by Ordnance Survey and made it on to OS maps, some have guidebooks, some may have websites, and some may be more modest affairs, walked not by the masses but by the few. But all these long-distance trails, official or otherwise, have emerged from grassroots endeavour and I praise them all.

CHAPTER 20

DEEPDALE

Nature

I'd originally intended to take three days to reach Catterick from my campsite in Weardale, having planned one overnight stop at Middleton-in-Teesdale and a second one south of Barnard Castle. In the end I decided to concertina things. I reached Middleton from Low Force not long after lunchtime and pushed on, deciding to do the remaining distance in a day and a half. I'd spotted on the map the campsite at Lartington run by the Camping and Caravanning Club, just at the right spot for a final night's stop. I made for there.

The Pennine Way had parted company from me again at Middleton but I had an alternative route to follow in the form of the Tees Railway Path. Just as in Peebles, an old railway line has been turned into a really delightful footpath and cycleway, one which slices its way through the countryside past the villages of Mickleton, Romaldskirk and Cotherstone. A few dog walkers were sharing the path with me, but otherwise all was quiet. The old station buildings at Romaldskirk and Cotherstone came and went (there is something evocative about disused rural stations). I crossed old viaducts and bridges and strolled through cuttings.

The Tees Railway Path took me almost to the edge of the village of Lartington before it petered out, and from there it was only a short distance further to walk. The campsite has the advantage that it is within walking distance of Barnard Castle, ideal for campers (like me) wanting to find something to eat since Lartington itself now has no shop or pub. But the campsite has in my opinion a second advantage and that is that it is only a stroll away from the Deepdale nature reserve.

Deepdale Beck is the little stream which runs almost due east at this point to meet the Tees just upstream from Barnard Castle. Deepdale

Wood, which embraces both sides of the beck and also extends up the valley of the smaller tributary stream Ray Gill, is an ancient semi-natural woodland which has been wooded for at least four hundred years and as such is today a haven for wildlife of all kinds. The woods which comprise the nature reserve are privately owned, but fate has found them the best possible kind of owner they could have acquired in the form of the professional ecologist John Durkin. Durkin, a former trustee of the Durham Wildlife Trust, clearly knows his woodland intimately. He has published a comprehensive guide to the flora in the reserve which he says totals about 400 species and which includes rare plants such as the Yellow Star of Bethlehem, the Bird's Nest Orchid, Toothwort and the Early Purple Orchid. Add in all the lichens, mosses, liverwort and fungi in the nature reserve and at least another 250 species can be added to the list.

What is commendable about the management of the nature reserve is the way that public access to the woods is actively encouraged. There's a good network of footpaths, one of which I noticed had been made accessible for wheelchair users. As in Eshiels Wood near Peebles, community engagement is central to the way the woodland is looked after. I found out later that there are regular 'Deepdale Friday' working parties where local volunteers can participate in tasks like clearing footpaths and digging ponds.

The history of nature conservation in Britain and in particular the development of nature reserves is one which has tended to be detached, or at least semi-detached, from the story of the outdoor movement. The two traditions have not always directly related to each other, and on occasions there has even been a little bit of mutual suspicion (are ramblers going to destroy important habitats? – are conservationists trying to restrict access to the countryside?). You could picture it like a pair of parallel tracks travelling through time, with the first containing the evolving story of national parks, long-distance trails and countryside access legislation, while on the other track would be the development of National Nature Reserves and the designation of important habitats as Sites of Special Scientific Interest, SPAs and SACs.

I started my account of the British access movement in the Pentland Hills, with Walter Smith and James Bryce. Where should an account of the British conservation movement start? The conventional point of departure would be the meeting called in May 1912 at London's Natural History Museum by the influential figure of Charles Rothschild, a member of the Rothschild banking family but also a passionate naturalist with a particular interest in entomology, the study of insects. Rothschild, at this stage in his early thirties, had two years earlier used some of his wealth to buy Woodwalton Fen, an area of a little over a hundred hectares of natural fenland in Cambridgeshire. His purchase was a precautionary measure to safeguard the habitat and to help protect the wildlife there. He was now keen to see this idea embraced by others. The meeting he called established a new organisation, the Society for the Promotion of Nature Reserves (SPNR), and under its auspices Rothschild led a working group which over the next five years identified 284 sites across Great Britain and Ireland which were deemed worthy of consideration for special protection as nature reserves.

The work of Rothschild and his colleagues was nothing if not comprehensive and the list of the sites they came up with is a fascinating one. It includes remote outliers like St Kilda and Foula, rather less distant islands such as Northumberland's Farne Islands and Lindisfarne, and a complete cross-section of mainland habitats from high montane to lowland heath. I would dearly love to be able to report that the 'Rothchild List' (as it has become known) also included John Durkin's woodlands in Deepdale but sadly history is not quite so obliging (although upper Teesdale north of Middleton most definitely does get on the List). What is interesting is how many of the places identified have now indeed become protected habitats, some of them as National Nature Reserves, some under the custodianship of the relevant local Wildlife Trust, and some through organisations such as the National Trust and the RSPB. Certainly in relation to the island of Great Britain if perhaps not Ireland there are very few of the 'Rothschild' sites which haven't over the past hundred years had some form of protection afforded them.

What was innovative about Charles Rothschild's SPNR was that it was calling for the protection of habitats rather than just focusing on individual species. Rothschild himself was to die in 1923 while only in his mid-forties, but some years before his death he made over the ownership of Woodwalton Fen to the young Society he had formed. It was the first reserve to be held by the SPNR, the organisation which (after several name changes over the years) is now known as The Wildlife Trusts and which brings together the more than forty separate regional and county wildlife trusts which have since sprung up in Britain.

It has to be said though that the concept of acquiring land as sanctuaries and reserves for nature can be traced back well before that 1912 meeting of Rothschild's. There is in any case surely a shared impulse here with an organisation like the Commons Preservation Society which was formed in 1865 and was responsible for saving (for people, but also for nature) such important London green spaces as Hampstead Heath and Epping Forest. The Commons Preservation Society later went on to include footpath protection work in its remit as well as helping to establish the National Trust (it is now the Open Spaces Society).

Perhaps we should guard against trying to separate too rigidly the early outdoor movement from its links with the study of natural history. After all, naturalists had to venture into the countryside to find and identify species, and naturalist Field Clubs with organised study trips were a feature of many towns in the nineteenth century. There was also the very particular phenomenon in that century of autodidact working-class natural historians in the manufacturing cities and towns of Lancashire and Yorkshire who would walk out from the mill towns where they had their employment into the neighbouring countryside to pursue their field studies. One such person was the Lancashire man Ernest Evans, born in the mid-1850s, who probably deserves to be better remembered than he is. He was first employed aged 13 as a carder in the town of Barnoldswick, he became a weaver, but then he went on later in life to write a very well-regarded botany textbook and to lead the natural science department at Burnley College. Tom Stephenson, long before he was writing articles on his Pennine Way proposal, was one of Evans' students. Evans "was a great rambler... a practical naturalist, making frequent field excursions," Stephenson recalled in his memoirs: "As one who studied under him and walked many miles with him, I learned much from his wide knowledge and his enthusiasm in the field". There is nothing necessarily incompatible between taking your recreation in the countryside and scientific endeavour.

Nevertheless the twentieth century did see a marked divergence of the ways. During the thirties, while the coalition which made up the Standing Committee on National Parks was busy lobbying hard for national parks and countryside access (page 90), the Society for the Promotion of Nature Reserves was separately trying to persuade the government to endorse the idea of nature reserves. For both groupings it took the war to put some momentum behind their efforts. 1941 saw the SPNR host an influential conference entitled *Nature Preservation in Post-War Reconstruction* and a year later came the welcome government decision to appoint an 'investigation committee' into the subject. The committee was charged with looking into how a network of reserves might be established, where they might be, and how they could be funded and administered. Some of the detailed work of identifying possible reserves was delegated to regional sub-committees to research (needless to say the 'Rothschild List' played a valuable role in this work).

Unlike the outdoor movement's more populist approach to lobbying, those pushing nature reserves and nature conservation tended to emphasise their scientific credentials. They perhaps also had the advantage of being closer to the British establishment in class terms than some of those active in ramblers' or youth hostelling groups.

Both these currents, however, were brought together by the post-war Labour government in the same piece of legislation, the National Parks and Access to the Countryside Act of 1949. This, as we've seen, represented for the outdoor movement in England and Wales a landmark change in the law but there was also a smaller part of the Act which covered nature reserves (and helpfully this part of the Act also applied to Scotland). The Act led to the creation of the concept of National Nature Reserves and of Sites of Special Scientific Interest under the remit of a new body called Nature Conservancy, later the Nature Conservancy Council. Today there are over two hundred national reserves in England (now looked after by Natural England), ranging in size from the thousands of hectares of the Wash estuary to a small quarry in Portland, Dorset. The independent regional and county Wildlife Trusts have their own reserves and there are also numerous less formal local nature reserves with differing ownership and management structures – one of which of course is Deepdale.

Scotland currently has 29 national nature reserves looked after by NatureScot, a small number of other national reserves managed by bodies such as National Trust Scotland and the RSPB, and a much larger number of reserves cared for by the Scottish Wildlife Trust. Wales has 76 national reserves, mostly administered by Natural Resources Wales. In each country the national nature reserves also tend to be designated as SSSIs and are also frequently given further SAC and SPA status.

It's quite a tally, more than Rothschild proposed. Eleven per cent of Britain's land mass is now designated formally as protected land for nature conservation purposes. You feel that Rothschild would be very encouraged at the way his idea has made it into reality. And yet…

And yet Britain today is "one of the most nature-depleted countries on Earth". This quotation comes from the State of Nature report for 2023, the latest in a series of rigorously researched studies from the State of Nature Partnership which has set itself the task of regularly assessing the numbers and distribution of wildlife in the United Kingdom. The production of the report is a significant operation, linking more than sixty organisations including conservation charities, research institutes and statutory nature conservancy bodies.

Their 2023 report is a sober read. It talks of a significant loss of diversity in Britain, with more species seeing their numbers decrease than increase. 16% of species are facing extinction from Britain, the report claims. 'Species' here covers the full range of flora and fauna, and the report among other things highlights the plight of insects. The distribution of invertebrates in the UK has gone down on average by 13% since 1970, with pollinating insects showing a larger decline (18%) and pest controlling insects down on average by 34%.

Not every species is on a downward trajectory: the State of Nature report found some that were increasing their numbers and distribution. But taken as a whole the picture is a negative one. The main causes according to the report are changes in the way that agriculture is using the land and the effects (already) of climate change. "If we are to halt and reverse biodiversity decline we need not only to increase our efforts towards conservation and restoration, but also to tackle the drivers of biodiversity loss, especially in relation to our food system," it argues.

The UK is not alone in experiencing a significant loss of biodiversity – it is a global phenomenon. Biodiversity is declining faster than at any time in human history. As the United Nations points out, we are experiencing the largest loss of life on our planet since the dinosaurs, with a million plant and animal species potentially threatened with extinction.

The UN's annual COP (Conference of the Parties) summits which are attempting to develop a global strategy to tackle climate change tend now to be covered in the mainstream media, helped perhaps by the 2021 conference being held in Glasgow. Rather less well publicised have been the parallel series of COP events focusing on the other great crisis facing humanity in our time, the loss of biodiversity.

However these COP Biological Diversity summits have been taking place under UN auspices broadly every two years since 1994. You can of course be sceptical as to what set-piece occasions like these can achieve in practice to reverse current trends. Nevertheless a potentially valuable agreement was made in 2022 at the COP15 in Montreal when representatives of 188 governments agreed what is called the Global Biodiversity Framework. This sets the goal of halting the process of the loss of nature by 2030 and of achieving nature recovery by 2050. Britain, as a participant at the COP summit, has committed to abide by the Framework.

So far, perhaps, so good. But how in Britain are we going to achieve the task of stemming the biodiversity loss we are experiencing? Protection is clearly part of the answer, and improving the quality of our existing protected lands would certainly be valuable. However the argument here would be that conservation by itself seeks simply to protect what is already present rather than helping bring back what we have lost. Protection is good but we also need ecological restoration.

One possible response which is being discussed goes by the name of nature-based solutions. This effectively means looking for ways for nature itself to do the heavy lifting, rather than trying to impose human answers. Perhaps one example could be how we can reduce flood risk by allowing our rivers to find again their meanders and water meadows rather than by sending in the diggers to dredge the river beds. Working with nature rather than against it does seem a pretty sensible tactic.

Another term that's much in fashion these days, a term you will have heard of, is rewilding. Several times on my walk it came up in conversation. Sometimes it brought negative comments: Dave and Annabel Stanners, for example, conjured up the prospect of invasive bracken and scrub taking over their farm land if it was allowed to be left just to natural forces.

The State of Nature 2023 report accepts that rewilding is potentially controversial: "it remains a contested concept that is applied to a wide variety of different practices," it explains. In fact, the controversy is probably there because there is as yet no widely accepted definition of what rewilding means. The International Union for Conservation of Nature has been working on a definition, but at the moment rewilding can be a slippery term. What does it imply? Does it mean withdrawing altogether from human intervention in the land and letting nature run its course? Does it necessarily have to include reintroducing predators which have long been extinct in Britain, such as wolves or lynx? Or is rewilding simply a conveniently media-friendly term for a range of measures which taken together can help us achieve biodiversity recovery?

My own quibble with the term, maybe, is primarily with those first two letters, 're-'. Rewilding implies returning to some previous version of the landscape, conjuring up a vision perhaps of a prelapsarian state of nature before humans messed things up. But as we've seen humans have been intervening in our land for millennia, almost since the time when the glaciers first retreated and the last Ice Age came to an end, and our lands today are moulded by all this past human activity. What sort of wildness are we thinking of restoring?

Having expressed my slight scepticism, it's fair to say that Rewilding Britain, the main advocacy organisation in the UK, offers a definition of rewilding that is inclusive of both nature and humanity. It calls for "a mosaic of species-rich habitats restored and connected across at least 30% of Britain's land and sea by 2030". At the same time it argues that such an approach would benefit Britain's people, offering "opportunities for communities to diversify and create more resilient, nature-based economies".

In Scotland the Scottish Rewilding Alliance is also sensitive to the idea that rewilding should support nature and people together. It calls for Scotland to declare itself a 'Rewilding Nation' and says that this would mean a country rich in wildlife, with hills covered with a tapestry of native woodlands and healthy peatlands. But such a country would also be "full of vibrant communities, where nature's restoration inspires and supports local enterprises, where people of all ages can find rewarding jobs..."

So let's return one final time to the economics behind all this. I argued earlier in this book that if we want to arrive at an understanding of the landscape we need to explore the economics of the way the land is used. I suppose if I wanted to propose a single 'take away' message from this book this would be it.

To assist me to understand the economics of what should be happening if we really try to tackle climate change and biodiversity loss I found the perfect mentor in the Cambridge economist Sir Partha Sarathi Dasgupta, or more precisely in the report *The Economics of Biodiversity* that he wrote for the British government in 2021, more commonly known simply as the Dasgupta Review. This is a massive piece of work coming in at over 600 pages, some of which is devoted to the more mathematical end of economics. But Dasgupta does have one very simple message in his report, and that is that we need to understand that we and our economic systems are necessarily 'embedded' in nature rather than conveniently external to it. "We are part of nature, not separate from it," Dasgupta affirms. This means that we need an approach to economic growth that acknowledges this.

Dasgupta points out that the usual measure of economic growth, gross domestic product, disregards nature. GDP makes no allowance for the depreciation of assets, he says, including the degradation of the natural environment. It's a tool that helps understand short-term economic output but it is unsuited to identifying investment and sustainable development and if we focus simply on GDP we are at risk of pursuing unsustainable economic growth.

This is an argument which, it seems to me, is far from being currently understood by the world's governments for whom GDP remains the primary indicator of 'growth'. But if we don't change our thinking, the prospects for both nature and humanity seem grim. Here is how Dasgupta summarises the options that we have: "Humanity faces an urgent choice. Continuing down our current path – where our demands on Nature far exceed its capacity to supply – presents extreme risks and uncertainty for our economies. Sustainable economic growth and development requires us to take a different path, where our engagements with Nature are not only sustainable, but also enhance our collective wealth and that of our descendants."

CHAPTER 21

CATTERICK BRIDGE

The lands we share

And so my walk comes to an end.

I have by this stage left the high ground a long way behind. My route from Barnard Castle takes me through a more pastoral landscape to Richmond where I meet up with my final river, the Swale. From Richmond I pass by one last impressive monastic ruin, that of Easby Abbey, and then it is simply a matter of a couple of miles' hike along a rather too-busy B-road to get to Catterick Bridge.

There isn't much there to greet me. The bridge itself used to be significant. It used to take the A1, the Great North Road, over the Swale. But today its role is very much diminished, usurped by the large concrete viaduct which I cross underneath a little way further upstream while above my head the traffic on the A1(M) is hurrying by.

I pause for a moment to read the interpretation board that's been erected on the river bank. Once upon a time, it tells me, Catterick was an important place. Once, long before Catterick was Catterick it was Cataractonium, the Roman settlement on the river bank where *their* main road north reached the Swale. Here for the first time since the Cheviots I am reunited again with Dere Street. Somewhere nearby, extremely close to the motorway viaduct, Dere Street travellers crossed the Swale.

The Romans chose a strategically important location for Cataractonium and the site developed into a sizeable town, playing a significant role in the regional economy for more than four hundred years, basically until the Romans had other things on their mind and decided to leave Great Britain to its own devices. What they left behind here has recently been extensively excavated as part of a very large archaeological exercise which took place when the dual carriageway A1 was being upgraded into the motorway. It was clearly a productive dig, with the photographic records showing extensive Roman remains being uncovered at Catterick Bridge literally feet away from where road-building equipment was at work building our modern highway.

The Romans were by no means the first to rearrange the landscape here, however. Evidence from the A1(M) dig, which was undertaken along the length of the motorway upgrade from Dishforth near Ripon up to Barton north of Scotch Corner, has extended archaeologists' understanding of the use of this land in prehistoric times. It has also reinforced the theory that there was an established routeway crossing the Swale hereabouts which had potentially been used for millennia. "To drive along the A1(M) through North Yorkshire is to experience a route that has been a conduit for travel, transportation and commerce for millennia," is the conclusion of the report of the archaeological dig, appropriately entitled *The Evolution of Dere Street from Routeway to Motorway*. As the report makes clear, evidence of life on these lands in pre-Roman times is ample.

In fact underneath the Army's Marne Barracks about three miles south of Catterick Bridge has been found what I suppose you could describe as a Neolithic factory. Five thousand years ago, give or take, people were working here turning flints into tools on a specially made floor constructed with cobbles. They left behind some of the rejected flint flakes, lying where they were discarded until archaeologists early this century brought them to light.

So when the Gododdin warriors (page 84) came to Catterick in their battle armour some time around 570 CE – if, that is, we go along with the idea that the location of Catraeth in the poem *Y Gododdin* is indeed Catterick – they were frankly coming to ground which had been well worked over by humans for a very long time before them. The age of mead-drinking and heroics in battle seems light years away from our own time and yet in terms of human history – let alone in terms of geological time – the lives they lived were, as it were, only yesterday. The Neolithic flint-knappers were occupying this land just the day before yesterday.

I try to explain in the first chapter of this book how I feel that the lands I have been walking through are 'shared'. But sharing land and landscapes is an activity through time, too, as one generation follows another. I've been conscious as I've slowly made my way south that

I have been sharing these lands with all those who came before me. These have been their lands too. The landscape today and the wealth we enjoy come from the interactions they had with the land. And we will be sharing the lands with future generations – or at least, let's hope that they will be here in due course to enjoy them. The way we run our economy seems predicated on short-termism but surely the longer view is necessary. As I've said several times in this book we have the issues of climate change and biodiversity loss which it is our responsibility to tackle, as part of what we leave as a legacy for the future.

There's something else: the lands we share stretch very much wider than the countryside I have been walking through, that little meandering line I have taken through a particular part of the island of Great Britain. We necessarily share the whole of our planet, and with it the responsibilities that go with looking after it.

There is a particular example I can offer, and it relates to the subject of peat degradation and restoration. In writing that chapter I drew on material published by the UK Centre for Ecology and Hydrology, including a useful factsheet on the subject which they have produced which summarises the key issues. The factsheet has much to say about the importance of peat in the context of British habitats, about the implications of peat loss in relation to greenhouse gas emissions, and about the action that is being taken to try to bring British peatlands back into a little better condition. But the leaflet also has a final section of six short paragraphs where it leaves the British situation behind and takes a global view. It concludes: "The issue of peatland degradation is most acute in the tropical peatlands of Southeast Asia, primarily in the islands of Borneo and Sumatra, where over two-thirds of all peat swamp forests have been cleared and drained since 1990... Much of this land has been converted to industrial palm oil and pulpwood plantations."

Relevant for us? I think so. The store cupboards in my kitchen demonstrate that palm oil is an ingredient in everyday food items that my family and I take for granted. Whether I want to or not, I surely have to share some responsibility for the loss of those peatlands of south-east Asia (and for the disappearance of the Sumatran tigers and the orangutans that the factsheet goes on to mention) as much as I do for our own peat-covered moors and for the plight of the beautiful hen harriers which should be flying over them in sizeable numbers – but aren't.

Those 200+ miles are now behind me as I stand on Catterick Bridge.

On my journey I've walked lands which were once the property of the Borders monasteries, often today forming part of the big estates of major aristocratic landowners. I've walked through countryside blighted by the eighteenth century Clearances. I've walked through commercial forestry plantations, and on land put aside for the Ministry of Defence. I've walked – but only for very short distances unfortunately – on land which is now in community ownership. And I have certainly made my way across countless farms, some where the land is owned by those who farm it and some where those who do the farming are just the current tenants.

Property is important in our society and the law is very particular about the subject. But I think I want to claim a different kind of stake in this land from that which is offered by title deeds. One of the academic papers I came across when looking at land reform questions in Scotland was by an anthropology lecturer at the University of Aberdeen. His paper talked among other things about the experience of walking the countryside. "Through their regular journeys and their familiarity with the hills, many walkers have already taken on a kind of ownership of the hills," he wrote. I think I want to claim this kind of ownership. By reading this book I think you too can claim it.

***

Catterick Bridge is the end of my journey. Except, of course, that it isn't. I take a selfie as I stand on the bridge and another photo from the bridge of the river Swale as it flows on downstream, just as it has flowed here for centuries. Then I cross the bridge to the south side, down to where Catterick Racecourse today covers much of the traces of Cataractonium. I need to find a bus stop in order to catch a bus to take me to Darlington station, where in turn I can catch a train to take me home.

The bus stop is two or three miles away, in one of the social housing estates close to the Army's big base at Catterick Garrison. I leave Catterick Bridge behind and carry on walking.

NOTES AND SOURCES

I've chosen not to weigh down this book with end notes or references. But I do have an obligation, I believe, to show the sources I have used in writing the chapters of this book and in making all the various assertions I have made.

So what follows is a list of the principal reference material which I have used. I have cast my net as widely as I can but undoubtedly some sources which I should have consulted will have escaped my attention. It's also the case that some of the issues explored (for example, land reform in Scotland and agricultural subsidies) are areas where developments are currently fast-moving, so there may have been changes in the time between this book going to press and you, the reader, finding it.

I have pondered how useful it would be to give full web addresses and have decided that my approach will be to include home page URLs for organisations and groups I reference. I also include longer website URLs where it may be less straightforward to find material online using a search engine (for example, Natural England reports on SSSI conditions are not particularly easy to locate). However where reports and documents can be readily found via an online search I simply advise you of this. (The website addresses listed were checked at time of publication.)

1: Making a start
European Landscape Convention: https://www.coe.int/en/web/landscape.

2: The right to wander
The best book I have come across on the story of the development of the British outdoor movement (including James Bryce's endeavours and the later campaigning for access rights) is *A Claim on the Countryside* by Harvey Taylor, Keele University Press, (1997).
Tom Stephenson's *Forbidden Land* (Manchester University Press) was published in 1989. Two years earlier came Marion Shoard's wide-ranging

This Land is Our Land: The struggle for Britain's countryside (Paladin, 1987). A little earlier again was Howard Hill: *Freedom to Roam: The struggle for access to Britain's moors and mountains* (Moorland Publishing, 1980).

Academic writings on access issues in Scotland which I have consulted included:

David L Carey Miller, 'Public Access to Private Land in Scotland', *Potchefstroom Electronic Law Journal/Potchefstroomse Elektroniese Regsblad* 15(2), August 2012.

Erling Berge and Lars Carlsson (eds.), *Commons: Old and New, Proceedings from a workshop*, Centre for Advanced Study, Oslo 11-13 March 2003, Norwegian University of Science and Technology (ISS Rapport No. 70).

Gregory S Alexander, *The Sporting Life: Democratic Culture and the Historical Origins of the Scottish Right to Roam*, Cornell Law School Legal Studies Research Paper Series No. 16-16, University of Illinois Law Review, 4/5 2016.

Jo Vergunst, 'Scottish Land Reform and the Idea of 'Outdoors'', *Ethnos*, 78(1), pp. 121–146 (2012).

The Scottish Paths Map is online at the Ramblers' website (https://www.ramblers.org.uk/). The Scottish Outdoor Access code is also online: https://www.outdooraccess-scotland.scot/.

ScotWays have several informative pages on their early history on their website www.scotways.com. The Friends of the Pentlands have an extensive website at https://pentlandfriends.org.uk/. The North Tweeddale Paths group also have a website: http://northtweeddalepaths.org.uk/.

The Pentland Hills Regional Park Strategic Management Plan 2019-2028 can be found online.

Christopher Harvie wrote the entry for 'James Bryce' in *The Oxford Dictionary of National Biography* (latest version 2011).

I bought online (somewhat randomly, because it was from a bookseller in Carmarthenshire) a copy of William Smith's slim little guidebook. It is from Walter Smith that I take the Walter Scott quotation about 'Cairnethy'.

3: Drovers

A R B Haldane's *The Drove Roads of Scotland*, originally published in 1953, has recently been brought back into print (2021) by Birlinn. Haldane's research has been extended by Richard Lowdon in his PhD thesis for the University of Glasgow *To travel by older ways: a historical-cultural geography of droving in Scotland* (2014). Lowdon's comprehensive account is available online. The description of droving being 'an undertaking that requires genius' is from W Leslie, *General View of the Agriculture of the Counties of Nairn and Moray* and is referenced by Lowdon.

K J Bonser, *The Drovers: Who they were and how they went: An epic of the English countryside* (1970) was originally published by Macmillan.

The reference to cattle carrying themselves to market is in Book 4, chapter 2 of Adam Smith's *Wealth of Nations* (1776).

The Walter Scott reference to drovers' fare is from his story *The Two Drovers* which is included in a collection of his short stories, *Chronicles of the Canongate, and* which is available in the Walter Scott Digital Archive, http://www.walterscott.lib.ed.ac.uk/etexts/.

For the UK Critical National Infrastructure see https://www.npsa.gov.uk/critical-national-infrastructure-0.

For more on the loss of the commons in Scotland and the Division of Commonties Act, see the booklet by Andy Wightman, Robin Callander and Graham Boyd, *Common Land in Scotland: A brief overview* (2003), as well as other writings by Andy Wightman.

The Supreme Court website https://www.supremecourt.uk/cases/uksc-2023-0126.html has information on the Dartmoor wild camping appeal by Alexander Darwell.

4: Community woodlands

Information about Eshiels Wood can be found at the group's Facebook page, https://www.facebook.com/EshielsW while the Peebles Community Trust website is https://peeblescommunity.org/. All the documentation submitted for the successful Eshiels asset transfer bid is still available at https://forestryandland.gov.scot/what-we-do/communities/community-empowerment-cats/previous-asset-transfer-requests/eshiels-wood-cats-application.

The Community Woodlands Association has much useful information available at its website, https://www.communitywoods.org/. Wooplaw's website is https://wooplaw.org/.

Information on the Tweed Railway Path is widely available, including at Sustrans' website.

Information about the Scottish Land Fund is here: https://www.tnlcommunityfund.org.uk/funding/programmes/scottish-land-fund.

5: Commercial forestry

Traquair House website: https://www.traquair.co.uk/.

For Walter Scott's *The Two Drovers* story see notes to chapter 3.

For the classic book on Scottish land clearances: T M Devine, *The Scottish Clearances* (Allen Lane, 2018).

Woodland Nation, written by Anna Lawrence and Willie McGhee, was published by the Forest Policy Group (https://www.forestpolicygroup.org/) in 2021. As well as this, the FPG's website contains much other material, including *Forest Ownership in Scotland 2022*, written by Andy Wightman and Jon Hollingdale.

The Borders Forest Trust website is: https://bordersforesttrust.org/.

The Cheviot, the Stag and the Black, Black Carbon was written by Alastair McIntosh and published by Community Land Scotland in 2023. Available online.

The group Reforesting Scotland (https://reforestingscotland.org/) publishes a regular eponymous magazine. The Spring/Summer 2023 edition included a feature by Theo Stanley, *Carbon finance: does it streamline Scottish woodland creation?*

An interesting report of a 2022 workshop on the implications of carbon offsetting for Scottish communities has been made available by the University of Strathclyde. The report, authored by M J Hannon and colleagues and available online, is entitled *Carbon Offsetting and Communities: Can Nature-Based Voluntary Carbon Offsetting Benefit Scottish Communities?* The website for the on-going project linked to this theme is: https://www.scottishinsight.ac.uk/Programmes/JustTransition/CarbonOffsetting.aspx.

The UK government agency Forest Research (https://www.forestresearch.gov.uk/) produces numerous publications, including the regular series of *Forestry Statistics* reports. Also from Forest Research is the little factsheet by James I L Morison, *Climate change and forests: How do woodlands and forests affect the climate?*

The economic contribution of the forestry sector in Scotland, from CJC Consulting, dates back to 2015. Scotland's government produced *Scotland's Forestry Strategy 2019-2029* in early 2019 (available online). Information on government grants in England, Scotland, Wales and N Ireland can be found here: https://www.gov.uk/guidance/tree-planting-and-woodland-creation-overview.

The Woodland Carbon Code home page (https://woodlandcarboncode.org.uk/) provides a link to the UK Land Carbon Register. The Broadmeadows case study can be found via a search on this site.

The asset managers Gresham House have a number of publications on forestry as an investment (https://greshamhouse.com/real-assets/forestry), which is where my 'proven asset class' quote comes from. Land and estate agents such as Strutt and Parker also regularly produce guides to the current market for commercial forestry and the land the trees sit on.

6: Land ownership

Alistair Moffat's *The Borders: A History of the Borders from Earliest Times* was originally published in 2002 by Deerpark Press and has been republished by Birlinn. Birlinn also publish his *The Reivers* (2007).

Andy Wightman's books and website are invaluable when it comes to issues of land ownership in Scotland. His books include *Who Owns Scotland* (Canongate, 1996) and *The Poor Had No Lawyers – who owns Scotland (and how they got it)* (Birlinn, new edition published 2024). A short update *Who Owns Scotland 2024* was recently made available online. Andy Wightman blogs regularly on land ownership and land reform issues (https://andywightman.scot/) and also runs the database website https://whoownsscotland.org.uk/.

Mention also needs to be made here of the work of Guy Shrubsole who has undertaken similar work to Andy Wightman in the English context. He is the author of *Who Owns England?: How We Lost Our Green and Pleasant Land, and How to Take It Back* (Collins, 2019). His excellent *The Lie of the Land* (HarperCollins) came out in late 2024, just as this book was being prepared for publication. He also runs, with Anna Powell-Smith, the blog *Who Owns England?* (https://whoownsengland.org/).

An earlier work on this issue is Kevin Cahill's *Who Owns Britain* (Canongate, 2001).

For a thought-provoking look at wider issues of land ownership across the globe, I recommend *Owning the Earth* by Andro Linklater (Bloomsbury, 2014).

The organisation which coordinates community land campaigning in Scotland is Community Land Scotland, whose website https://www.communitylandscotland.org.uk/ is full of valuable material. The 'Lamborghini' quote is referenced in CLS's *Land for the Common Good – Manifesto for a Sustainable Scotland* (2020)

A short essay on the Scottish land issue by Mike Danson and Craig Dalzell, *Land Ownership and Community Development*, is included in *A New Scotland* (ed. Gregor Gall, Pluto Press, 2022).

My quote from Mairi Gougeon MSP is from the government's press release in March 2024, https://www.gov.scot/news/land-reform-bill/. The response from Scottish Land and Estates can be found online. Andy Wightman has perceptive blogs on the same subject.

The newspaper I reference from the time of the 2003 Land Reform Act ("Albania of northern Europe") was the Daily Mail.

The Bowhill website is https://www.bowhillhouse.co.uk/ and the Buccleuch landholdings are detailed online at https://www.buccleuch.com/land-registration/buccleuch-land-ownership/.

The Langholm Initiative has more information at https://www.langholminitiative.org.uk/.

Although I don't cover the topic in my chapter, there has been very welcome work undertaken recently on Scottish estate and land ownership in relation to wealth generated from slavery, using the *Legacies of British Slavery* database developed by University College London (https://www.ucl.ac.uk/lbs/project/details/). The 2020 report by Iain MacKinnon and Andrew Mackillop, *Plantation slavery and landownership in the west Highlands and Islands: legacies and lessons* was published by Community Land Scotland and is available from their website (above). Iain MacKinnon followed this up with a short blog on the Bella Caledonia blog site: https://bellacaledonia.org.uk/. The National Records of Scotland offer information for researchers on this subject: https://www.nrscotland.gov.uk/research/learning/slavery.

7: Tam Lin

The Child ballads have been published over the years in many editions and have also more recently been digitised. One place to find the collection is https://www.gutenberg.org/ebooks/author/38603.

Scott's *Minstrelsy of the Scottish Border* has likewise been digitised (for example, http://www.bookrags.com/ebooks/12882/46.html#20&gsc.tab=0). Scott's mention of the Cheese Well comes in his lengthy essay in the book which introduces the Tam Lin ballad, *On the fairies of popular superstition.*

The text of *The Scots Musical Museum* has also been made available online: https://imslp.org/wiki/The_Scots_Musical_Museum_(Folk_Songs,_Scottish).

The Ballad and the Folk by David Buchan was first published in 1972 by Routledge and Kegan Paul, and has since been reissued by Tuckwell Press.

Scottish Fairy Belief was published by Tuckwell Press in 2001, and has since been reissued by John Donald/Birlinn.

Academic writings consulted include:

Martha Hixon, 'Tam Lin, Fair Janet and the Sexual Revolution', *Marvels and Tales*, Vol. 18, No. 1 (2004), pp. 67-92.

Lynn Wollstadt, 'Controlling Women: Reading Gender in the Ballads Scottish Women Sang', *Western Folklore*, Vol. 61, No. 3/4 (Autumn 2002), pp. 295-317.

Gretchen Kay Lutz, *The Feminine Corpus in F.J. Child's Collection of the English and Scottish Popular Ballads*, (thesis, Rice University, 1998).

Lucie Duggan, 'A woman's tradition? Quantifying gender difference in the Child ballads', *Orbis Litterarum*, Vol. 78, Issue 5 (Oct. 2023), open access at https://onlinelibrary.wiley.com/doi/10.1111/oli.12400.

8: Rivers, floods

Information about the various flood risks and alleviation schemes in the Tweed valley can be accessed from this SEPA webpage: https://www2.sepa.org.uk/frmstrategies/tweed.html. The report on the proposals for the Selkirk scheme was taken to the Scottish Borders Council meeting on 24 Nov. 2011. Information on the situation in Hawick is at https://www.hawickfloodscheme.com/.

Details of the river Tweed SSSI and SAC designations can be found at the NatureScot website, https://www.nature.scot.

The River Tweed Commission website is https://rivertweed.org.uk/.

9: Waiting for the train

David Spaven's comprehensive book *Waverley Route: The battle for the Borders Railway* was published in 2012 by Argyll Publishing. The third edition (2017) is from Stenlake Publishing.

Peter Heubeck, 'Resurrecting Railways: Lessons from two Scottish projects', *PWI Journal*, Vol. 141, Part 1 (Jan. 2023), pp. 34-42.

The Campaign for Borders Rail website: https://campaignforbordersrail.org/.

10: The dark side of history
Trimontium Trust museum: https://www.trimontium.co.uk/.
Roman Britain website: https://www.roman-britain.co.uk/places/newstead/.
The full report by James Curle on his dig at Trimontium, *A Roman Frontier Post and its People*, originally published in 1911 by the Society of Antiquaries in Scotland, has been republished and digitised by the Trimontium Trust, available at https://curlesnewstead.org.uk/pdfs/curle.pdf.
The report of the 2002 dig at Eildon Hill North by James O'Driscoll and Gordon Noble (University of Aberdeen), *Eildon Hill North – Data Structure Report*, is also available in digital form from the Trimontium Trust website.
Historic Environment Scotland has a detailed entry for Eildon Hill North: https://canmore.org.uk/site/55668/eildon-hill-north.
Walter Scott's referencing of Thomas the Rhymer is in his *Minstrelsy of the Scottish Border* (see above). James Hogg's story 'The Hunt of Eildon' is one of the stories in *Tales and Sketches by the Ettrick Shepherd*, published by William P Nimmo in Edinburgh in 1883. It has been digitised at https://archive.org/details/talesandsketche07hogggoog.
The Survey of Scottish Witchcraft database and website, held by the University of Edinburgh, is at https://witches.hca.ed.ac.uk/. This site has a comprehensive 'further reading' bibliography and an informative FAQ section. The database and map for *Places of Residence of Accused Witches in Scotland* is at https://witches.is.ed.ac.uk/.
Christina Larner's pioneering book, *Enemies of God: the Witch-Hunt in Scotland* was published by Chatto and Windus in 1981.
A much more recent book is that from Mary W Craig, *Borders Witch Hunt* (Luath Press, 2020).
Relevant academic papers on Scottish witch-hunts consulted include:
W H Neill, 'The Professional Pricker and His Test for Witchcraft', *The Scottish Historical Review*, Vol. 19, No. 75 (Apr. 1922).
Julian Goodacre, 'Women and the Witch-Hunt in Scotland', *Social History*, 23, (Oct. 1998), pp. 288-308.
The witches of Scotland campaigning group has a website: https://www.witchesofscotland.com/about.

11: War and Strife
There are several archaeological records held for different sections of Dere Street on the Historic Environment Scotland database. The search tool can be accessed at https://canmore.org.uk/site/search.
The story of the 'debatable land' is central to Graham Robb's book of the same name, published in 2018 by Picador.
There is much information on the so-called 'Dark Ages' in the Borderlands in the thesis by Ian Mervyn Smith for the University of Durham *The*

archaeological background to the emergent kingdoms of the Tweed Basin in the Early Historical period. The thesis is available from the university: http://etheses.dur.ac.uk/1431/.

Among other material I consulted on this period of history are these books by Celtic scholars:

Kenneth Jackson, *Language and History in Early Britain*, published by Edinburgh University Press, 1953.

Nora Chadwick, *The British Heroic Age, the Welsh and the Men of the North*, University of Wales Press (Cardiff), 1976.

Brynley F Roberts (ed.), *Early Welsh Poetry: studies in the Book of Aneirin*, published by the National Museum of Wales (Aberystwyth), 1988.

Among the various translations of *Y Gododdin* are these key texts:

Kenneth Jackson, *The Gododdin*, Edinburgh University Press, 1969.

A O H Jarman, *Aneirin: Y Gododdin, Britain's oldest heroic poem*, published by Gomer, 1988.

John T Koch, *The Gododdin of Aneirin, Text and Context from Dark-Age North Britain,* University of Wales Press (Cardiff), 1997.

For Gillian Clarke's fine translation of *Y Gododdin* into English poetry: *The Gododdin: Lament for the Fallen*, published by Faber in 2021.

Academic and other writings on *Y Gododdin* are numerous. I consulted among others:

John T Koch, 'The Place of 'Y Gododdin' in the History of Scotland', *Celtic Connections: Proceedings of the Tenth International Congress of Celtic Studies,* Vol. 1, pp. 199-210.

Tim Clarkson, 'The Gododdin Revisited' (review of Koch's 1997 book), *The Heroic Age*, Issue 1, Spring/Summer 1999.

One of those authors critical of the Catraeth=Catterick theory is Craig Cessford. See his essay 'Yorkshire and the Gododdin Poem' in *Yorkshire Archaeological Journal,* Vol. 68, 1996, pp. 241-243.

12: National parks

For information on the Roman site at Pennymuir, see https://www. roman-britain.co.uk/places/pennymuir/ and https://canmore.org. uk/site/83741/pennymuir. For information on the Chew Green archaeological site, see https://historicengland.org.uk/listing/the-list/ list-entry/1015847.

The reports to government mentioned in this chapter are:

(The Dower report): *National Parks in England and Wales,* May 1945, HMSO, Cmd. 6628.

(The Hobhouse report): Report of the National Parks Committee (England and Wales), July 1947, HMSO, Cmd. 7121.

(The Nugent report): Report of Defence Lands Committee 1971-1973, 1973, HMSO, Cmnd. 5714.

(The Glover report): Landscapes Review – final report, available online.

The 1938 CPRE film can be found here: https://www.youtube.com/ watch?v=-fd2cCKISBA.

I consulted various academic papers on the subject of national parks, including:

John Sheail, 'The concept of National Parks in Great Britain 1900-1950', *Transactions of the Institute of British Geographers,* No. 66 (Nov. 1975), pp. 41-56.

R W Hoyle, 'Opposition to the creation of national parks: the case of the Yorkshire Dales', *Agricultural History Review,* 67, II (2019) pp. 283-314.

The Campaign for National Parks published the report *National Parks and the Climate Emergency* in June 2021, available from its website https://www.cnp.org.uk/.

The Northumberland National Park website is https://www.northumberlandnationalpark.org.uk/. The Revere project: https://revere.eco/.

13: Upland farming

Information on the pearl mussels of the rivers Rede and Tyne can be found on various websites, including https://www.revitalisingredesdale.org.uk/projects/river-rede-improvements/the-need-for-action/. The Environment Agency website for their Salmon Centre at Kielder is: https://www.visitkielder.com/nature-wildlife/kielder-salmon-centre-kielder.

Alfred Wainwright mentions the local ramblers' proposal to take the Pennine Way along the Rede riverbank in his *Pennine Way Companion* (first edition published by Westmorland Gazette, 1968).

A good starting place for information on agricultural grants in England is the Defra website https://www.gov.uk/guidance/funding-for-farmers. The equivalent site for Scotland is https://www.ruralpayments.org/topics/all-schemes/. Welsh agricultural grants are outlined at https://www.gov.wales/rural-grants-payments.

Health and Harmony: the future for food, farming and the environment in a Green Brexit was published by Defra in Feb. 2018, Cm. 9577. It has been overtaken by later events but nevertheless is still available online.

Working together for a thriving agricultural tenanted sector, The 'Rock Review', (Oct. 2022) is available online. My data for farm tenancies in England comes both from the Rock Review and from more recent Defra statistics (also available online). Only a small minority of farms are wholly tenanted (14% in England) but there are many more farms (31%) which are partly owner-occupied but partly also operating on tenanted land. About 54% of farms in England are fully owner-occupied. The percentage of farms operating on a *wholly* tenanted basis (such as the Stanners' farm in Redesdale) is particularly high in the North-East at 22% of all farms and these wholly tenanted farms represent 29% of actual farmland.

The Nature-Friendly Farming Network website: https://www.nffn.org.uk. For Dave and Annabel's converted railway carriage: https://wanniesretreat.co.uk/. Alan Simpson's blog: https://www.alansimpson.org.uk/blog/.

14: Boundaries

English Heritage has a webpage on Brocolitia and the temple of Mithras. There is also a separate webpage with information specifically on the Mithras cult. Both can be found using a search engine.

W H Auden's *Collected Poems* were brought out in an edition by Faber in 1976 (revised 1991), edited by Edward Mendelson.

Information relating to Hadrian's Wall's acceptance as a World Heritage Site by Unesco is available here: https://whc.unesco.org/en/list/430/.

Anita Sethi, *I Belong Here*, published by Bloomsbury, 2021.

15: Grouse moors

Hexham Abbey's website for visitors https://www.hexhamabbey.org.uk/ includes information on the abbey's history.

A Wainwright, *A Pennine Journey*, was published by Michael Joseph in 1986 and by Penguin a year later. It has recently been reissued by The Wainwright Society.

Blanchland village has a community website https://www.blanchland.org/. The Lord Crewe's Charity website is at https://www.lordcrewescharity. org.uk/. The charity's submission to Parliament in 2016 opposing the banning of driven grouse shooting can be found at https://committees. parliament.uk/writtenevidence/72094/html/.

Adrian Blackmore's account for the Countryside Alliance of his day's shooting at Blanchland: https://www.countryside-alliance.org/resources/ news/a-promising-start-to-the-glorious-twelfth.

The RSPB regularly publishes *Birdcrime*, an analysis of the persecution of wild birds, https://www.rspb.org.uk.

Mark Avery's account of the issues associated with grouse shooting, *Inglorious: Conflict in the Uplands*, was published by Bloomsbury in 2015. Mark has a blog, https://markavery.info/blog/. Wild Justice, https:// wildjustice.org.uk/, published a short report on the lack of monitoring of SSSI conditions in 2023, *A Sight for Sore SSSIs* (available online). Revive, the Scottish coalition for grouse moor reform, also has a website, http:// www.revive.scot/.

The problems in the implementation of the recent Scottish legislation is covered in a Guardian article *Scottish conservation agency accused of undermining law to protect birds of prey*, 14 November 2024.

Detailed information on the Muggleswick and Blanchland SSSI, including the original citation and reports of inspections, are on Natural England's website: https://designatedsites.naturalengland.org.uk/SiteDetail.aspx?Si teCode=S2000173&SiteName=Muggleswick&countyCode=&responsible Person=&SeaArea=&IFCAArea.

16: Water catchment

John Hassan's *A History of Water in Modern England and Wales* was published by Manchester University Press in 1998.

A short historical overview from Ofwat and Defra, *The Development of the Water Industry in England and Wales*, can be found online.

The National Infrastructure Commission published its report *Preparing for a drier future: England's water infrastructure needs* in 2018 (available online). The water industry is also tackled in the NIC's *The Second National Infrastructure Assessment* published in 2023, also available online.

A 2022 statement from Ofwat *Safeguarding the water supply for the future* and (also from 2022) the Environment Agency's *Review of England's emerging regional water resources plans* are available online.

For an anti-privatisation take on the water industry: https://weownit.org.uk/public-ownership/water.

17: Quarrying and mining

On the geology of Heights Quarry: https://www.mindat.org/loc-4761.html.

The planning officer's report to committee on the Heights Quarry extension: https://democracy.durham.gov.uk/documents/s109642/Heights%20Quarry%20and%20Extension.pdf.

Books and publications on lead mining:

C J Hunt, *The economic and social conditions of lead miners in the Northern Pennines in the eighteenth and nineteenth centuries* (thesis for Durham University, 1968, available online). The thesis formed the basis of Hunt's subsequent book, *The Lead Miners of the North Pennines*, published by Manchester University Press in 1970.

Arthur Raistrick and Bernard Jennings, *A History of Lead Mining in the Pennines*, published by Longmans 1965, reprinted by Davis Books and George Kelsall Publishing, 1983. This is the first comprehensive scholarly book on the subject.

Arthur Raistrick and Arthur Roberts, *The Life and Work of the Northern Lead Miner*, Alan Sutton Publishing, 1990. Primarily a collection of photographs but with an extended introduction.

Arthur Raistrick, The Lead Industry of Wensleydale and Swaledale, Vol. 1: The Mines, Moorland Publishing, 1991.

R A Fairbairn, *Weardale Mines*, British Mining monographs, No. 56, 1996. From the same author, *The Mines of Upper Teesdale*, British Mining monographs, No. 77, 2005.

Rookhope Primary School closure news story: https://www.bbc.co.uk/news/articles/c28ljk3gk4xo.

The song 'Fourpence a Day' can be found in various collections of songs (with varying orthography!), including in A L Lloyd (compiler) *Come All Ye Bold Miners: Ballads and Songs of the Coalfields*, Lawrence and Wishart, 1952.

Museums: Killhope Museum website: https://killhope.org.uk/. Weardale Museum: https://weardalemuseum.org.uk/.

18: Peat

For *A Pennine Journey* see notes for chapter 15.

The Wainwright Society: https://www.wainwright.org.uk/. The Pennine
Journey Supporters Club: https://penninejourney.org/pjsc/.

Maps of UK peatlands:

England: https://naturalengland-defra.opendata.arcgis.com/maps/45c40ddec
8d42ea95c6d0a77e74f442.

Scotland: see https://www.nature.scot/professional-advice/planning-
and-development/planning-and-development-advice/soils/
carbon-and-peatland-2016-map.

Wales: https://datamap.gov.wales/maps/peatlands-of-wales-maps/.

Government and government agency reports on peat issues:

UK Government, *England Peat Action Plan*, 2021, available online.

Natural England, *Carbon storage and sequestration by habitat – A review of the
evidence*, 2021, available online.

Natural England, *England's peatlands – carbon storage and greenhouse gases*,
2010, available online.

Other reports and studies on peat issues:

Matt Aitkenhead et al., *Peatland restoration and potential emissions savings
on agricultural land: an evidence assessment*, 2021, published by Climate
Exchange, available online.

IUCN UK: *Forest to Bog Restoration, Demonstrating Success*, 2024, available
online.

Tim Thom et al. *Conserving Bogs: The Management Handbook*, n.d., available
online.

Rebekka Artz et al., *The State of UK Peatlands: an update* commissioned by
IUCN UK Peatland Programme's Commission of Inquiry on Peatlands,
2019, available online.

Rebekka Artz et al., *Peatland restoration – a comparative analysis of the costs
and merits of different restoration methods*, Final Report, 2018, published
by Climate Exchange, available online.

Chris Evans et al., *Implementation of an emission inventory for UK peatlands*,
UK Centre for Ecology and Hydrology, 2017. Available online.

UK Centre for Ecology and Hydrology, *Peatlands factsheet*, at https://www.
ceh.ac.uk/sites/default/files/Peatland%20factsheet.pdf.

IUCN, Peatland Code, at https://www.iucn-uk-peatlandprogramme.org/
peatland-code-0.

Guy Shrubsole, *Who owns our carbon?*, Who Owns England?, 2021, see
https://whoownsengland.org/wp-content/uploads/2021/11/who-owns-
our-carbon-nov-2021.pdf.

Other peat restoration initiatives, websites:

Peatland ACTION (NatureScot): https://www.nature.scot/climate-change/
nature-based-solutions/peatland-action; North Pennines PeatLIFE,
https://bit.ly/peatlife; Great Northern Bog, https://greatnorthbog.org.
uk/; Moors for the Future, https://www.moorsforthefuture.org.uk/.

19: Long distance walking

For Alfred Wainwright's *Pennine Way Companion* see notes to chapter 13 and
for his *A Pennine Journey* the notes to chapter 15.

For Tom Stephenson's *Forbidden Land* see notes to chapter 2. His *Wanted:
A Long Green Trail* article was published in the Daily Herald on 22 June
1935.

The relevant correspondence between Stephenson and Royce on
the Pennine Way proposal is in the London Archives in folder
LMA/4287/02/398. Other relevant material can be found in folders
/02/399, /02/395/1 and /02/397.

For the Hobhouse report, see notes to chapter 12

Andrew McCloy's *The Pennine Way: The Path, the People, the Journey*,
contains much fascinating information. It was published by Cicerone in
2016.

20: Nature

The Deepdale website is https://www.durhamnature.co.uk/deepdale.
html. The Wildlife Trusts website is https://www.wildlifetrusts.org/.
Rothschild's List can be found here: https://www.wildlifetrusts.org/
about-us/rothschilds-list.

Harvey Taylor includes a chapter on working class rambler-naturalists in *A
Claim on the Countryside* (see notes for chapter 2). I also consulted *The
Naturalist in Britain, A Social History* by David Elliston Allen (Allen
Lane, 1976).

The *State of Nature Report 2023* is available online.

The Dasgupta report *The Economics of Diversity* is available online, as is
a shorter *Abridged Version*. Also online is the government's July 2021
response to the report.

The then-Conservative government issued a 25 year strategy for nature in
2018, *A Green Future: Our 25 Year Plan to Improve the Environment*. This is
available online.

A number of reports can be found at the Rewilding Britain website, https://
www.rewildingbritain.org.uk/ including the 2024 report *Rewilding
Finance*. The Scottish Rewilding Alliance website is https://www.rewild.
scot/.

21: The lands we share

English Heritage's website on Cataractonium has useful information and a
map showing the extent of the Roman site: https://historicengland.org.
uk/listing/the-list/list-entry/1021181?section=official-list-entry

The report *The Evolution of Dere Street from Routeway to Motorway* is by
David W Fell and Paul G Johnson and is available online.

For the UK Centre for Ecology and Hydrology's *Peatlands factsheet* see notes
to chapter 18.

The academic paper I quote from is that by Jo Vergunst. See notes to
chapter 2.

ACKNOWLEDGEMENTS

My grateful thanks to all those who helped me with this book, and particularly those who were prepared to be interviewed: Mark Avery, Gethin Chamberlain, Charles Dundas, Peter Heubeck, Paul Leadbitter, Maria McArdle and the Weardale Museum staff, Andrew McCloy, Donald McPhillimy, James Robinson, Andy Rockall, Laurence Rose, Jane Rosegrant, Marion Short, Annabel Stanners, Dave Stanners, Eileen Steinbock, Andy Wightman, Alex Wilson, John Woollams. I hope that, even if they do not necessarily share my views and assertions, they feel their views have been adequately represented. Any errors that may be in the text are of course my own responsibility.

Thank you to my other colleagues at Gritstone Publishing. I also need to pay tribute to Gillian Lonergan's methodical and meticulous copy-editing work. Finally, my thanks as always to Jane Scullion for her support, both during my walk and during the writing of this book.

THE ROUTE

Day 1. By train to Edinburgh. Edinburgh castle – Edinburgh campsite. About 4.3 miles.

Day 2. Edinburgh campsite – West Linton. About 17 miles.

Day 3. West Linton – Glentress. About 17.2 miles.

Day 4. Glentress – Selkirk. About 18.8 miles.

Day 5. Selkirk – Melrose. About 8 miles.

Day 6. Melrose – Jedburgh. About 17 miles.

Day 7. Jedburgh – Byrness. About 20 miles.

Day 8. Byrness – Bellingham. About 15.5 miles.

Day 9. Bellingham – Hexham. About 20.5 miles.

Day 10. Hexham – Edmundbyers. About 16 miles.

Day 11. Edmundbyers – Westgate. About 13 miles.

Day 12. Westgate – Lartington. About 20.1 miles.

Final day. Lartington – Catterick Bridge. About 22.6 miles. Bus to Darlington. Train home.

INDEX